Deleting "elect" in the Bible
THE COMPANION

A reasonable historical case for removal
of the word "elect" in the English Bible

Also by Jacques More

Will there be Non-Christians in heaven?
Leadership is Male?
So you think you're chosen?
Revival - The Battleplan
Serious Mistranslations of the Bible
Deleting "elect" in the Bible
Pink or Blue

Deleting "elect" in the Bible
THE COMPANION

A reasonable historical case for removal
of the word "elect" in the English Bible

By Jacques More

JAROM BOOKS

Cover design by
Grange Graphics Ltd - JN Creative

Printed by Latimer Trend

www.jarom.net

To David Pawson

David is a bible teacher and author of many books

PASSAGES AFFECTED

Ref.	OT Hebrew	KJV
2 Samuel 21:6	BACHIR	choose
1 Chronicles 16:13	BACHIR	chosen
Psalm 89:3	BACHIR	chosen
Psalm 105:6	BACHIR	chosen
Psalm 105:43	BACHIR	chosen
Psalm 106:5	BACHIR	chosen
Psalm 106:23	BACHIR	chosen
Isaiah 42:1	BACHIR	elect
Isaiah 43:20	BACHIR	chosen
Isaiah 45:4	BACHIR	elect
Isaiah 65:9	BACHIR	elect
Isaiah 65:15	BACHIR	chosen
Isaiah 65:22	BACHIR	elect
	NT Greek	
Matthew 20:16	*EKLEKTOS*	chosen
Matthew 22:14	*EKLEKTOS*	chosen
Matthew 24:22	*EKLEKTOS*	elect
Matthew 24:24	*EKLEKTOS*	elect
Matthew 24:31	*EKLEKTOS*	elect
Mark 13:20	*EKLEKTOS*	elect
Mark 13:22	*EKLEKTOS*	elect
Mark 13:27	*EKLEKTOS*	elect
Luke 18:7	*EKLEKTOS*	elect
Luke 23:35	*EKLEKTOS*	chosen
Romans 8:33	*EKLEKTOS*	elect
Romans 16:13	*EKLEKTOS*	chosen
Colossians 3:12	*EKLEKTOS*	elect
1 Timothy 5:21	*EKLEKTOS*	elect
2 Timothy 2:10	*EKLEKTOS*	elect
Titus 1:1	*EKLEKTOS*	elect
1 Peter 1:2 (Gk. 1:1)	*EKLEKTOS*	elect
1 Peter 2:4	*EKLEKTOS*	chosen
1 Peter 2:6	*EKLEKTOS*	elect
1 Peter 2:9	*EKLEKTOS*	chosen
2 John 1:1	*EKLEKTOS*	elect
2 John 1:13	*EKLEKTOS*	elect
Revelation 17:14	*EKLEKTOS*	chosen

CONTENTS

Preface 10

The Challenge 12

The Evidence List 16

How did the first Christians read these passages? 18
BACHIR and *EKLEKTOS*

How did the first Christians read *EKLEKTOS*? 30
First example of every Hebrew word

More than just one example 46

Then there are doubts to examine 64

Doubts examined more closely 89

Other historical pointers 105

So how should we translate BACHIR and *EKLEKTOS* 111

Conclusion 132

What you can do 135

List of Bible Passages 137

PREFACE

Deleting ELECT in the Bible (DEiTB) is the title of an exhaustive work of reference comprising of every passage where each of 24 Hebrew words are found; All those 24 words were translated by the Greek word *EKLEKTOS* in the bible of the first Christians. This Greek version of the bible which Jesus and the apostles quote in the New Testament (NT) is known as the Septuagint (LXX). Those 24 Hebrew words occur 594 times in the Old Testament (OT) and in the LXX are translated by *EKLEKTOS* on 74 occasions. This means 594 full quotes in DEiTB.

EKLEKTOS is the only Greek word from which "elect" is translated in the English bible. It is also used to translate "chosen": (being) "selected" is the idea of both those English words. The Old Testament (OT) has "elect" only translated from the Hebrew word BACHIR. This Hebrew word BACHIR is also only translated in the LXX by *EKLEKTOS*. So *EKLEKTOS* fully understood provides a true picture as to whether "elect" (selected/chosen) is a valid meaning both for *EKLEKTOS* and BACHIR.

The related Greek word *EPILEKTOS* not found in the NT, but also in the LXX occurs 11 times. So that by being exhaustive *Deleting ELECT in the bible* adds those 11 to the 594 mentioned above and provides the reader with over 600 passages quoted in the English of the Hebrew text translated; with the Greek of the LXX in every case, an English interlinear of that and, with various other English versions literal or liberal whenever found appropriately needful for each text. This makes DEiTB a comprehensive work useful for research and easy recognition. With the analysis and introduction as only 15% of the space of the book and 85% the source reference mentioned, much of the title "**reads like a telephone book**" (David Pawson) to most readers. Hence the need for something a little smaller: Something accessible for everyone who does not wish or need to see all of the source material completely, but still obtain a true and full picture.

This shorter book was at first going to be named *Deleting ELECT in the Bible – The Short Version*. But, by adding a chapter on different ways to render the Hebrew and Greek passages affected by the mistranslation and, by adding a new introduction and other comments, this shorter work is much more than just a summary or synopsis of the exhaustive *Deleting ELECT in the bible*.

I am calling it *Deleting ELECT in the Bible – The Companion*.

Deliberately, very few abbreviations have been used in *The Companion*: As well as reducing the New Testament to "NT" and the Old Testament to "OT", the Septuagint is referred to by "LXX", the English translation of the LXX by Sir Lancelot as "engLXX" and, *Deleting ELECT in the Bible* as "DEiTB".

Where words in Greek and Hebrew appear, they have been given in the manner I first observed used by Robert Young in his concordance: using capital letters in English for both Hebrew and Greek words. The Hebrew words are not italicised. The Greek letters are Anglicised as follows:

Anglicised Greek letter Chart

A	A-α	Alpha	*B*	B-β	Bēta	*G*	Γ-γ	Gamma
D	Δ-δ	Delta	*E*	E-ε	Epsīlon	*Z*	Z-ζ	Zēta
É	H-η	Ēta	*TH*	Θ-θ	Thēta	*I*	I-ι	Iōta
K	K-κ	Kappa	*L*	Λ-λ	Lambda	*M*	M-μ	Mu
N	N-ν	Nu	*X*	Ξ-ξ	Xī	*O*	O-o	Omīcron
P	Π-π	Pī	*R*	P-ρ	Rhō	*S*	Σ-ς,σ	Sigma
T	T-τ	Tau	*U*	Υ-υ	Upsīlon	*PH*	Φ-φ	Phī
CH	X-χ	Chī	*PS*	Ψ-ψ	Psī	*Ó*	Ω-ω	Ōmega
H	Refers to grave accent (`) present over an initial vowel/s of a word in the Greek							

The Challenge

Jesus mentioned the world of people to his disciples like this,

> . . . **lift up your eyes and look at the fields, for they are already white for harvest!**
> *John 4:35*

Paul wrote,

> **God . . . desires all men to be saved and to come to the knowledge of the truth.**
> *1 Timothy 2:3-4*

God is ready, the fields are ready, but Jesus also said,

> **The harvest truly *is* plentiful, but the laborers *are* few. Therefore pray the Lord of the harvest to send out laborers into His harvest.**
> *Matthew 9:37-38*

God is ready, the fields are ready, but the labourers, the Church, is that ready?

There is division in the Church caused by doctrine which the Lord hates (Revelation 2:15; 1 Timothy 4:1). There are whole groups of believers determined to stay separate and largely, some of these, are recognised due to a central doctrine commonly known as Calvinism. This has other names like "Reformed doctrine" and "Grace Theology". Two examples of these in the UK are the FIEC group of churches and the Grace Baptist churches. You cannot be accepted as a full member of these assemblies unless you hold to their beliefs over and above root Christian basic statements of faith like the Apostle's Creed. To this has been added the doctrine that only those God has "chosen" whom they call "the elect", only these will God save. A limit has been put on whom God loves and whom Jesus died for and this limiting spirit carries over into the action of whom they worship with regularly. It goes on. All who are not "elect", God has in effect, chosen to be lost and are damned forever. And, should witnessing about Jesus omit this doctrine, to them this means a false gospel is being preached. These grievous things are a living fact of Today's Church, the world of Christians. Wherever this dogma of Calvinism has reached, it has been a cause of division among Christians and division is a hindrance to witnessing and revival.

Calvinism is the doctrine that underpinned the basis for apartheid in South Africa with the Dutch Reformed church established in the country[1]. Calvin taught that nothing happens by chance and every act and event was decreed by God[2], so not only are few saved by God's choice, but to be black is to be chosen as a sub race group. That was the thinking behind this horror, even if this facet of practice was held only by a minor section of Calvinists worldwide.

These church members are taught that Calvinism is in the bible. But, they ignore the history of doctrine that shows the bible was never read like this for about 4 centuries. There was no such dogma of an unconditional predestination to salvation for individuals until the late writings, in the 5th century, of Augustine of Hippo. All John Calvin did in the 16th century was to re-teach Augustine, who was the one who introduced it to Christianity. Independent historians like Professor George Park Fisher make clear that before Augustine, this was not the view: his summary following his quotes on free will and associated is that "**conditional predestination is the doctrine inculcated** - what was persistently taught - **by the Greek Fathers.**"[3].

The bible of the first centuries was the Greek version of the OT with the letters and gospels of the apostles also written in Greek. This dogma was not read within the Greek within its use of the day. Today's bibles however do not give this opportunity: today's translations support this false dogma with the world "elect" in place and various passages with words re-arranged that lend support to the dogma.

So this Calvinist doctrine is supported by words, phrases and whole passages given as valid translations in today's bibles. This is far from the truth. In this book, the evidence is here in a more accessible form than its exhaustive predecessor. But, both these books show in full that there is no valid historical place for the word ELECT in the bible.

There are no elect.

So the question of the moral integrity is thereby raised of bible word gatherers in lexicons, of bible translators and of bible publishers in the continued unwarranted support of this doctrine. And though this book is about the translation of two words, "elect" and "chosen" from the OT Hebrew word BACHIR and the NT Greek word *EKLEKTOS*, as mentioned, whole phrases and sentences are also involved. A good example of this is seen if we compare Robert Young's literal translation of 1 Peter 1 with a more common version:

> **Peter, an apostle of Jesus Christ, to the choice sojourners of the dispersion of Pontus, Galatia, Cappadocia, Asia, and Bithynia, according to a fore-knowledge of God the Father, in sanctification of the Spirit, to obedience and sprinkling of the blood of Jesus Christ: Grace to you and peace be multiplied!**
>
> *1 Peter 1:1-2 YLT*

In contrast, the repeated re-ordering of the words in most translations gives support for the Calvinist idea.
Like this,

> **Peter, an apostle of Jesus Christ,**
> **To the pilgrims of the Dispersion in Pontus, Galatia, Cappadocia, Asia, and Bithynia, elect according to the foreknowledge of God the Father, in sanctification of the Spirit, for obedience and sprinkling of the blood of Jesus Christ:**
> **Grace to you and peace be multiplied.** *1 Peter 1:1-2*

In the second version we read of the "**elect according to the foreknowledge of God**", a good sound byte for Calvinism; but a clear divergence from the Greek which Young follows closely. I provide a Greek-English interlinear of this passage which helps show this at a quick glance in the exhaustive DEiTB and here in *The Companion* in a later chapter (Page 110). I also explain how the foreknowledge mentioned in 1 Peter 1 actually refers to the means of salvation being foreknown; not the individuals (Pages 126-128). In that ending chapter I provide examples of a better rendering for all the affected passages which currently use either "chosen" or "elect" from the Hebrew word BACHIR in the OT or the Greek word *EKLEKTOS* in the NT. One challenge then is to be true and accurate in translation with words and passages to convey the same meaning as was read and understood by the first Christians and only then to obtain one's doctrine from that; not the other way around: not to translate according to one's doctrine.

It must be remembered that the devil in tempting Jesus in the desert (Matthew 4 & Luke 4), he used the scripture. Jesus' replies also using scripture shows us that the devil used the very scripture text out of context. This is what teaching demons do (1 Timothy 4:1): they take portions of passages out of context, string them together, and impose these on the thought life of believers. These spirits vex Christians into believing error. There is no question of integrity on the part of the believer here, whether a new Christian or a mature teacher of the bible: that is, unless they in turn, then refuse to look afresh and do not do like the Bereans who were commended **"they received the word with all readiness, and searched the Scriptures daily to find out whether these things were so"** (Acts 17:11). Indeed all Christians after a time should realise that they have to re-learn things. This is because in one thing or another, we all get deceived, to whatever extent. It is a fact of life[4]. The trick is not to refuse to unlearn: to always be teachable; not gullible. There is a difference.

So, here is the evidence that "elect" should not be in the bible. Check it out for yourself, for that is your challenge.

[1] See *Taken on Trust* by Terry Waite
[2] *Institutes of Christian Religion* by John Calvin Book 1 Ch. 16 Sect. 4
[3] *History of Christian Doctrine* by George Park Fisher DD LLD
Pages 164-165
[4] See *Pink or Blue* by Jacques More – An autobiographical look at how deception operates

THE EVIDENCE LIST

Let's begin with the list. Here are the 74 places in the Septuagint (LXX) where *EKLEKTOS* can be found directly translating a Hebrew word. It is this source that enables an independent observation of what *EKLEKTOS* meant to the translators who compiled the LXX. We can thus not only observe how they viewed *EKLEKTOS*, but thereby also recognise this is the reasonable way it was understood by Greek readers.

In LXX
74 places where *EKLEKTOS* translates 24 Hebrew (Heb.) words

LXX		OT	Heb. word	LXX		OT	Heb. word
Genesis	23:6	=	MIBCHAR	Psalm	88:20	89:19	BACHAR
Genesis	41:2	=	BARI	Psalm	104:6	105:6	BACHIR
Genesis	41:4	=	BARI	Psalm	104:43	105:43	BACHIR
Genesis	41:5	=	BARI	Psalm	105:5	106:5	BACHIR
Genesis	41:7	=	BARI	Psalm	105:23	106:23	BACHIR
Genesis	41:18	=	BARI	Psalm	140:4	141:4	MANAMMIM
Genesis	41:20	=	BARI	Proverbs 8:19		=	BACHAR
Exodus	14:7	=	BACHAR	Proverbs12:24		=	CHARUTS
Exodus	30:23	=	DEROR	Song of Songs 5:15		=	BACHAR
Numbers	11:28	=	BECHURIM/BECHUROTH	Song of Songs 6:8		6:9	BAR
Deuteronomy 12:11		=	MIBCHAR	Song of Songs 6:9		6:10	BAR
Judges	20:15	=	BACHAR	Isaiah	22:7	=	MIBCHAR
Judges	20:34	=	BACHAR	Isaiah	22:8	=	NESHEQ
1 Samuel	24:3	24:2	BACHAR	Isaiah	28:16	=	BOCHAN
1 Samuel	26:2	=	BACHAR	Isaiah	42:1	=	BACHIR
2 Samuel	21:6	=	BACHIR	Isaiah	43:20	=	BACHIR
2 Samuel 22:27 (a)		=	BARAR	Isaiah	45:4	=	BACHIR
2 Samuel 22:27 (b)		=	BARAR	Isaiah	49:2	=	BARAR
1 Kings	4:23	=	BARI	Isaiah	54:12	=	CHEPHETS
2 Kings	8:12	=	BACHUR	Isaiah	65:9	=	BACHIR
2 Kings	19:23	=	MIBCHOR	Isaiah	65:15	=	BACHIR
1Chronicles 7:40		=	BARAR	Isaiah	65:23	65:22	BACHIR
1Chronicles 9:22		=	BARAR	Jeremiah 3:19		=	CHEMDAH/CHAMUDOTH
1Chronicles 16:13		=	BACHIR	Jeremiah 10:17		=	MATSOR
Ezra	5:8	=	GELAL	Jeremiah 22:7		=	MIBCHAR
Nehemiah 5:18		=	BARAR	Jeremiah 31:15		48:15	MIBCHAR
Psalm	17:27 (a)	18:26	BARAR	Jeremiah 32:34		25:34	CHEMDAH/CHAMUDOTH
Psalm	17:27 (b)	18:26	BARAR	Lamentations 1:15		=	BACHUR
Psalm	77:31	78:31	BACHUR	Lamentations 5:13		=	BACHUR
Psalm	88:4	89:3	BACHIR	Lamentations 5:14		=	BACHUR

LXX	OT	Heb. word	LXX	OT	Heb. word
Ezekiel 7:20	=	TSEBI	Ezekiel 31:16	=	MIBCHAR
Ezekiel 7:22	=	TSAMMERETH	Daniel 11:15	=	MIBCHAR
Ezekiel 19:12	=	PERI	Amos 5:11	=	MASETH
Ezekiel 19:14	=	PERI	Habakkuk 1:16 =		BARI
Ezekiel 25:9	=	TSEBI	Haggai 2:7		= CHEMDAH/CHAMUDOTH
Ezekiel 27:20	=	CHOPHESH	Zechariah 7:14 = CHEMDAH/CHAMUDOTH		
Ezekiel 27:24	=	BEROMIM	Zechariah 11:16 =		BARI

In DEitB I mention 91 places in the LXX where *EKLEKTOS* is found. My beginning list was found in Morrish's concordance of LXX. He lists 89 places. I found two more, but could not find 6 of his in the LXX text used. 10 times *EKLEKTOS* was used by the LXX authors without reference to a Hebrew word being translated. And 1 was *EPILEKTOS*, another word. This leaves 74 directly translated from a Hebrew word. The 24 Hebrew words and the English renderings for them are our independent witness to the meaning of *EKLEKTOS*.

How did the first Christians read these passages?
BACHIR and *EKLEKTOS*

I mentioned previously the two words from which "elect" is found in today's English bibles, the Hebrew word BACHIR in the OT and the Greek word *EKLEKTOS* in the NT. The reason the NT was written in Greek was that after Alexander the Great conquered the known world and, after his 4 successors among whom the Greek empire was then divided (all prophesied in Daniel), the world continued in using Greek as the language of administration. This went on well until the next big conquering empire, that of the Romans, for whom Latin was their lead language. This meant that in Israel, Mediterranean nations and the Middle East, the known civilised world, Greek was the main language of interaction for trade and administration. This was right up until the 4th century AD as Latin then took over and that mainly in the West of the Roman Empire. A good example of this known interaction in Greek among the first Christians is the fact that the proceedings of the first ecumenical Church council held in Nicea in 325AD (now Iznik in Turkey) was conducted and recorded in Greek. This was the first gathering of church leaders from all over the Roman Empire. A time when as yet there were no main divisions among Christians, as well as a recognition existing, of independence from each other of various church jurisdictions of the empire: mutually recognised and recorded. Greek was a unifying factor and the scriptures of both the OT and the NT were read in Greek.

When we read the NT we find quotes are made by Jesus and the apostles from the OT. These quotes are not from the Hebrew Original text of the OT, but from the Greek Version of the OT. This Greek translation as a tradition, as recorded by the Jewish historian Josephus, is given as carried out in Alexandria by 72 Jewish scholars invited to the task. Hence the common name for the Greek version of the

OT: The Septuagint (LXX). These OT quotes in English bibles can often be seen to differ in detail from the OT passages read directly. This is because the Greek Version, the LXX was not always as accurate and the OT in our modern languages is translated directly from the Hebrew.

Here is Jesus quoting the LXX

Matthew 4:10

Jesus said to the Devil in the wilderness:

> **Away with you, Satan! For it is written, '*You shall worship the* LORD *your God, and Him only you shall serve.*'**
> *Matthew 4:10*

The LXX contains the words *KAI AUTÓ MONÓ* in English "***and Him only***", and this "*only*" translated from Deuteronomy 6:13 is not found in the Hebrew.

Because our OT is translated from the original Hebrew the word "*only*" cannot be read in the OT passage of our modern bible. As we can see:

> **You shall fear the** LORD **your God and serve Him, and shall take oaths in His name.** *Deuteronomy 6:13*

The word "*only*" is not there. This vouches therefore for Matthew and Jesus' use of the LXX. It vouches for Luke too, who quotes Jesus saying the same thing against the Devil "***and Him only you shall you serve***" (Luke 4:8).

Here is Paul quoting the LXX

Romans 12:19-20

> **Beloved, do not avenge yourselves, but *rather* give place to wrath; for it is written, '*Vengeance is Mine, I will repay,*' says the Lord. '*Therefore if your enemy hungers, feed him; if he thirsts, give him a drink; for in so doing you will heap coals of fire on his head.*'** *Romans 12:19-20*

This latter OT quote is direct from Proverbs 25:21-22. The Greek is exactly the same in the LXX as the NT text, whilst in the Hebrew text and our Bibles Proverbs 25:21-22 reads,

> **If your enemy is hungry, give him bread to eat; and if he is thirsty, give him water to drink; for *so* you will heap coals of fire on his head . . .**
> *Proverbs 25:21-22*

Paul makes no mention of "**bread**" or "**water**" but it is clearly there in the Hebrew. Equally he mentions "*in so doing*" which is in the LXX and nowhere in the Hebrew.

I also give examples for John and Peter in DEiTB.

It is this version of the OT, the LXX, which was read directly by Christians for at least three centuries alongside the letters and gospels that make up the NT. So that in reading and appreciating this Greek literature, the early Christians held the same meaning for words in the OT and the NT. For bible translators today this makes the LXX a primary source for understanding and obtaining a true meaning for Greek words found in the NT. This has tragically not been practised. The very purpose of this book you are reading is to show, to demonstrate, that this prime source for appreciating words in Greek, the LXX, as been left unrecognised by the many. Robert Young is a rare exception. He investigated the meaning of every word used in the bible autographs in the Hebrew and the Greek. This is seen by his concordance of words in the bible and his literal version of the bible (see the later chapter *Other historical pointers*).

Allow me then to get on with it, to show you that *EKLEKTOS* is the word to be looked at and then to show how this was read by the early Church.

First let's show that every instance of BACHIR in the OT is given by *EKLEKTOS* in the LXX. We then know that *EKLEKTOS* represents the meaning for both those source words.

Here follows the simple list, then a quote of each passage in full, so the reader is fully equipped to see the truth: BACHIR is fully and only represented by *EKLEKTOS* in the LXX.

This is the list of all places in the OT where BACHIR is found along with the given translation from the KJV.

2 Samuel 21:6	BACHIR	choose
1 Chronicles 16:13	BACHIR	chosen
Psalm 89:3	BACHIR	chosen
Psalm 105:6	BACHIR	chosen
Psalm 105:43	BACHIR	chosen
Psalm 106:5	BACHIR	chosen
Psalm 106:23	BACHIR	chosen
Isaiah 42:1	BACHIR	elect
Isaiah 43:20	BACHIR	chosen
Isaiah 45:4	BACHIR	elect
Isaiah 65:9	BACHIR	elect
Isaiah 65:15	BACHIR	chosen
Isaiah 65:22	BACHIR	elect

Here they are again, quoted in full (NKJV the default bible version in *The Companion*), with the LXX translation, my interlinear, and an English translation of the LXX by Sir Lancelot (engLXX). This shows these are the correct passages and that *EKLEKTOS* is the only Greek word used by the LXX translators to depict BACHIR.

2 Samuel 21:6 BACHIR

> let seven men of his descendants be delivered to us, and we will hang them before the LORD in Gibeah of Saul, *whom* the LORD **chose**." And the king said, "I will give *them*."

LXX 2 Kings 21:6

[In the LXX 1 Samuel = 1 Kings, 2 Samuel = 2 Kings, 1 Kings = 3 Kings & 2 Kings = 4 Kings]

DOTÓ HÉMIN HEPTA ANDRAS EK TÓN HUIÓN AUTOU
  give   us   seven   men out of the sons   of him

KAI EXÉLIASÓMEN AUTOUS TÓ KURIÓ EN TÓ
 and we shall hang   them to the Lord in the

*GABAÓN SAOUL **EKLEKTOUS** KURIOU KAI EIPEN HO*
  Gabaon of Saul   choice   of Lord and said the

BASILEUS EGÓ DÓSÓ
    king   I shall give

engLXX

Let one give us seven men of his sons, and let us hang them up in the sun to the Lord in Gabaon of Saul, as chosen out for the Lord. And the king said, I will give *them*.

---

1 Chronicles 16:13 BACHIR

O seed of Israel His servant, you children of Jacob, **His chosen ones!**

LXX

SPERMA ISRAÉL PAIDES AUTOU HUIOI IAKÓB
  seed   of Israel | of him   sons of Jacob
                young servants

EKLEKTOI *AUTOU*
  choice   of him

engLXX

ye seed of Israel his servants, *ye* seed of Jacob his chosen ones.

Psalm 89:3 BACHIR

"I have made a covenant **with My chosen**, I have sworn to My servant David:

LXX Psalm 88:3

*DIETHEMÉN DIATHÉKÉN TOIS **EKLEKTOIS** MOU*
  ordained   covenant with the   choice   of me

ÓMOSA DAUID TÓ DOULÓ MOU
  sworn   David the servant of me

engLXX

> I made a covenant with my chosen ones, I sware unto David
> my servant.

Psalm 105:6 BACHIR

**O seed of Abraham His servant, you children of Jacob, His
chosen ones!**

LXX Psalm 104:6

SPERMA ABRAAM DOULOI AUTOU HUIOI IAKÓB
   seed of abraham servants of him   sons of Jacob

EKLEKTOI *AUTOU*
   choice   of him

engLXX

> *ye* seed of Abraam, his servants, *ye* children of Jacob, his
> chosen ones.

Psalm 105:43 BACHIR

**He brought out His people with joy, His chosen ones
with gladness.**

LXX Psalm 104:43

KAI EXÉGAGE TON LAON AUTOU EN AGALLIASEI KAI
 and   led out   the people of him in   exultation and

*TOUS **EKLEKTOUS** AUTOU EN EUPHROSUNÉ*
  the   choice   of him in   gladness

engLXX

> And he brought out his people with exultation, and his chosen
> with joy;

Psalm 106:5 BACHIR

That I may see the benefit of **Your chosen ones**, that I may rejoice in the gladness of Your nation, that I may glory with Your inheritance.

LXX Psalm 105:5

*TOU IDEIN EN TÉ CHRÉSTOTÉTI TÓN **EKLEKTÓN***
the to see in the gracious of the choice

SOU TOU EUPHRANTHÉNAI EN TÉ EUPHROSUNÉ TOU
of you of the to be glad in the gladness of the

ETHNOUS SOU TOU EPAINEISTHAI META TÉS
nations of you of the praise with the

KLÉRONOMIAS SOU
Inheritance of you

engLXX

that we may behold the good of thine elect, that we may rejoice in the gladness of thy nation, that we may glory with thine inheritance.

Psalm 106:23 BACHIR

Therefore He said that He would destroy them, had not Moses **His chosen one** stood before Him in the breach, to turn away His wrath, lest He destroy *them*.

LXX Psalm 105:23

KAI EIPE TOU EXOLOTHREUSAI AUTOUS EI MÉ
and said of the to utterly destroy them if not

*MÓUSÉS HO **EKLEKTOS** AUTOU ESTÉ EN TÉ*
Moses the choice of him stood in the

THRAUSEI ENÓPION AUTOU TOU APOSTREPSAI APO
breach before him of the to turn from

THUMOU ORGÉS AUTOU TOU MÉ EXOLOTHREUSAI
raging anger of him of the not to utterly destroy

engLXX

> So he said that he would have destroyed them, had not Moses his chosen stood before him in the breach, to turn him away from the fierceness of his anger, so that he should not destroy them.

Isaiah 42:1 BACHIR

> "Behold! My Servant whom I uphold, **My Elect One** *in whom* My soul delights! I have put My Spirit upon Him; He will bring forth justice to the Gentiles.

LXX

> *IAKÓB HO PAIS MOU ANTILÉPSOMAI AUTOU ISRAÉL*
> Jacob   the | of me   shall take hold   of him   Israel
>   young servant
>
> *HO **EKLEKTOS** MOU PROSEDEXATO AUTON HÉ*
> the   choice   of me   accepted   him   the
>
> *PSUCHÉ MOU EDÓKA TO PNEUMA MOU EP AUTON*
> soul   of me   gave   the   spirit   of me upon   him
>
> *KRISIN TOIS ETHNESIN EXOISEI*
> judgment to the nations shall bring forth

engLXX

> Jacob is my servant, I will help him: Israel is my chosen, my soul has accepted him; I have put my Spirit upon him; he shall bring forth judgement to the Gentiles.

Isaiah 43:20 BACHIR

> The beast of the field will honor Me, the jackals and the ostriches, because I give waters in the wilderness and rivers in the desert, to give drink to My people, **My chosen**.

LXX

> *EULOGÉSOUSI ME TA THÉRIA TOU AGROU SEIRÉNES*
> shall bless   me the wild beasts of the field   sirens

KAI THUGATERES STROUTHÓN HOTI EDÓKA EN TÉ
and   daughters   of ostriches since gave in the

ERÉMÓ HUDÓR KAI POTAMOUS EN TÉ ANUDRÓ
desert   water and   rivers   in the waterless

*POTISAI TO GENOS MOU TO **EKLEKTON***
to water the race of me the   choice

engLXX

the beasts of the field shall bless me, the owls and young ostriches; for I have given water in the wilderness, and rivers in
the dry land, to give drink to my chosen race,

Isaiah 45:4 BACHIR

For Jacob My servant's sake, and Israel **My elect**, I have
even called you by your name; I have named you, though
you have not known Me.

LXX

HENEKEN TOU PAIDOS MOU IAKÓB KAI ISRAÉL TOU
for the sake of the | of me Jacob and Israel of the
        young servant

***EKLEKTOU** MOU EGÓ KALESÓ SE TÓ ONOMATI SOU*
  choice   of me I   call you with the name of you

KAI PROSDEXOMAI SE SU DE OUK EGNÓS ME
 and   accept   you you but not known me

engLXX

For the sake of my servant Jacob, and Israel mine elect, I will
call thee by thy name, and accept thee: but thou hast not
known me.

Isaiah 65:9 BACHIR

I will bring forth descendants from Jacob, and from Judah
an heir of My mountains; **My elect** shall inherit it, and My
servants shall dwell there.

LXX

> *KAI EXAXÓ TO EX IAKÓB SPERMA KAI EX IOUDA KAI*
> and lead out the out of Jacob seed   and out of Juda and

> *KLÉRONOMÉSEI TO OROS TO HAGION MOU KAI*
> shall inherit   the mountain the holy of me and

> *KLÉRONOMÉSOUSIN HOI **EKLEKTOI** MOU KAI HOI*
> shall inherit   the   choice   of me and the

> *DOULOI MOU KAI KATOIKÉSOUSIN EKEI*
> servants of me and   they shall dwell   there

engLXX

> And I will lead forth the seed *that came* of Jacob and of Juda,
> and they shall inherit my holy mountain: and mine elect and
> my servants shall inherit it, and shall dwell there.

Isaiah 65:15 BACHIR

**You shall leave your name as a curse to My chosen; for
the Lord GOD will slay you, and call His servants by another
name;**

LXX

> *KATALEIPSETE GAR TO ONOMA HUMÓN EIS*
> shall leave behind for the   name   of you into

> *PLÉSMONÉN TOIS **EKLEKTOIS** MOU HUMAS DE ANELEI*
> satiety   to the   choice   of me you but take up

> *KURIOS TOIS DE DOULEUOUSI MOI KLÉTHÉSETAI*
> Lord   to the but   serve   to me shall be called

> *ONOMA KAINON*
> name   new

engLXX

> For ye shall leave your name for a loathing to my chosen, and
> the Lord shall destroy you: but my servants shall be called by
> a new name,

Isaiah 65:22 BACHIR

They shall not build and another inhabit; they shall not plant and another eat; for as the days of a tree, *so shall be* the days of My people, and **My elect** shall long enjoy the work of their hands. 23They shall not labor in vain...

LXX = Isaiah 65:22-23a

OU MÉ OIKODOMÉSOUSI KAI ALLOI ENOIKÉSOUSI KAI
in no wise   build   and others   dwell in   and

OU MÉ PHUTEUSOUSI KAI ALLOI PHAGONTAI KATA
in no wise   shall plant   and others   eat   according to

GAR TAS HÉMERAS TOU XULOU TÉS ZÓÉS ESONTAI
for   the   days   of the   tree   of the life   shall be

HAI HÉMERAI TOU LAOU MOU TA GAR ERGA TÓN
the   days   of the people of me the   for   works of the

*PONÓN AUTÓN PALAIÓSOUSIN 23 HOI **EKLEKTOI***
effort   of them   shall grow old   the   choice

MOU OU KOPIASOUSIN EIS KENON . . .
of me not they shall labour into void

engLXX

They shall by no means build, and others inhabit; and they shall by no means plant, and others eat: for as the days of the tree of life shall be the days of my people, they shall long enjoy the fruits of their labours. 23My chosen shall not toil in vain . . .

This was all the verses in English where BACHIR was found and all of them were translated by *EKLEKTOS* in its various declensions - *EKLEKTOUS; EKLEKTOI; EKLEKTOIS; EKLEKTOI; EKLEKTOUS; EKLEKTÓN; EKLEKTOS; EKLEKTOS; EKLEKTON; EKLEKTOU; EKLEKTOI; EKLEKTOIS; EKLEKTOI* – all these are declensions of the one word *EKLEKTOS*. And it is evident thereby *EKLEKTOS* is the only word used by the LXX translators for the Hebrew word BACHIR.

I said,

> "Allow me then to get on with it, to show you that *EKLEKTOS*
> is the word to be looked at and then to show how this was read
> by the early Church."

The 1st part is done: I have shown that *EKLEKTOS* is the word to be looked at. Every occasion that BACHIR is given, it was only translated by *EKLEKTOS* in the LXX. The LXX translators thereby reveal that to them these two words BACHIR and *EKLEKTOS* are indistinguishable in meaning. You may also have noticed Sir Lancelot, in his translation of the LXX (the "engLXX"), he assumes "elect" and "chosen" is a valid translation of *EKLEKTOS*. As we shall see this is the later "practise" of translating which we are now looking to see if true.

Let's now look at how *EKLEKTOS* was read by the early Church.

How did the first Christians read *EKLEKTOS*?

First example of every Hebrew word

We saw how BACHIR is only translated by *EKLEKTOS* and this occurs 13 times (X13). Since *EKLEKTOS* occurs X74 directly translating 24 different Hebrew words, this leaves us with 61 from 23 Hebrew words to give us the independent picture. In this chapter I will share the 23 all once with the undisputed main rendering for *EKLEKTOS*.

In alphabetical order all the Hebrew words translated by *EKLEKTOS* in the LXX are:

BACHAR, BACHIR, BACHUR, BAR, BARAR, BARI, BECHURIM/ BECHUROTH, BEROMIM, BOCHAN, CHARUTS, CHEMDAH/ CHAMUDOTH, CHEPHETS, CHOPHESH, DEROR, GELAL, MANAMMIM, MASETH, MATSOR, MIBCHAR, MIBCHOR, NESHEQ, PERI, TSAMMERETH, TSEBI

Now, in order of appearance in the bible, let's first give one example from each of the Hebrew words consistent with the top quality, the main thrust, excluding BACHIR (see previous chapter).

Remember the first quote is the Hebrew word translated in the NKJV, then the LXX translation of the Hebrew, a basic interlinear of the LXX, then Sir Lancelot's translation in English of the LXX.

Genesis 23:6 MIBCHAR (1-23)

> Hear us, my lord: You *are* a mighty prince among us; bury your dead in the **choicest** of our burial places. None of us will withhold from you his burial place, that you may bury your dead.

LXX

    5*KURIE* 6*AKOUSON DE HÉMÓN BASILEUS PARA THEOU*
    Lord   hear   but   us   king   by   God

    *SU EI EN HÉMIN EN TOIS **EKLEKTOIS** MNÉMEIOIS*
    you are in   us   in the   choice   tombs

    HÉMÓN THAPSON TON NEKRON SOU OUDEIS
    of us   entomb   the   dead   of you not one

    GAR HÉMÓN OU MÉ KÓLUSEI TÓ MNÉMEION AUTOU
    for   of us in no wise withhold for the tomb   of him

    APO SOU TOU THAPSAI TON NEKRON SOU EKEI
    from you of the to entomb the   dead   of you there

engLXX

    but hear us; thou art in the midst of us a king from God; bury thy dead in our choice sepulchres, for not one of us will by any means withhold his sepulchre from thee, so that thou shouldest not bury thy dead there.

Genesis 41:2 BARI (2-23)

    Suddenly there came up out of the river seven cows, fine looking and **fat**; and they fed in the meadow.

LXX

    KAI IDOU HÓSPER EK TOU POTAMOU ANEBAINON
    and   look   even as out of the   river   came up

    *HEPTA BOES KALAI TÓ EIDEI KAI **EKLEKTAI** TAIS*
    seven   oxen   fair to the sight and   choice with the

    SARXI KAI EBOSKONTO EN TÓ AXEI
    flesh   and   grazing   in the sedge

engLXX

    And lo, there came up as it were out of the river seven cows, fair in appearance, and choice of flesh, and they fed on the sedge.

Exodus 30:23 DEROR (3-23)

"Also take for yourself quality spices—five hundred *shekels* of **liquid** myrrh, half as much sweet-smelling cinnamon (two hundred and fifty *shekels*), two hundred and fifty *shekels* of sweet-smelling cane,

Take thou also unto thee principal spices, of **pure** myrrh five hundred *shekels*, and of sweet cinnamon half so much, *even* two hundred and fifty *shekels*, and of sweet calamus two hundred and fifty *shekels*,   *KJV*

LXX

KAI SU LABE HÉDUSMATA TO ANTHOS SMURNÉS
and you take   spices   the   flower   myrrh

EKLEKTÉS PENTAKOSIOUS SIKLOUS KAI
   choice   five hundred   shekels · and

KINNAMÓMOU EUÓDOUS TO HÉMISU TOUTOU
   cinnamon   fragrant   the   half   of this

DIAKOSIOUS PENTÉKONTA KAI KALAMOU EUÓDOUS
   two hundred   fifty   and   calamus   fragrant

DIAKOSIOUS PENTÉKONTA
   two hundred   fifty

engLXX

Do thou also take sweet herbs, the flower of choice myrrh five hundred shekels, and the half of this two hundred and fifty shekels of sweet-smelling cinnamon, and two hundred and fifty shekels of sweet-smelling calamus,

---

Numbers 11:28 BECHURIM/BECHUROTH (4-23)

So Joshua the son of Nun, Moses' assistant, *one* of his **choice men**, answered and said, "Moses my lord, forbid them!"

And Joshua the son of Nun, the servant of Moses, *one* of his **young men**, answered and said, My lord Moses, forbid them.
                                                        KJV

LXX

KAI APOKRITHEIS IÉSOUS HO TOU NAUÉ HO
and   answered   Jesus   the of the Naue who

PARESTÉKÓS MÓUSÉ HO **EKLEKTOS** *EIPE KURIE MÓUSÉ*
stood beside Moses the   choice   said Lord   Moses

KÓLUSON AUTOUS
prevent   them

engLXX

And Joshua the son of Naue, who attended on Moses, the chosen one, said, My lord Moses, forbid them

---

2 Samuel 22:27 BARAR (5-23)

With the pure You will show Yourself pure; and with the devious You will show Yourself shrewd.

LXX 2 Kings 22:27

[In the LXX 1 Samuel = 1 Kings, 2 Samuel = 2 Kings, 1 Kings = 3 Kings & 2 Kings = 4 Kings]

KAI META **EKLEKTOU EKLEKTOS** *ESÉ KAI META*
and with   choice   choice   I shall be and with

STREBLOU STREBLÓTHÉSÉ
crooked   crooked

engLXX

and with the excellent thou wilt be excellent, and with the froward thou will be froward.

---

2 Kings 8:12 BACHUR (6-23)

And Hazael said, "Why is my lord weeping?" And he answered, "Because I know the evil that you will do to the children of Israel: Their strongholds you will set on fire, and their **young men** you will kill with the sword; and you will dash their children, and rip open their women with child."

LXX 4 Kings 8:12

> *KAI EIPEN AZAÉL TI HOTI HO KURIOS MOU KLAIEI*
> and   said   Azael why since the Lord   of me weeps
>
> *KAI EIPEN HOTI OIDA HOSA POIÉSEIS TOIS HUIOIS*
> and   said since saw as many as shall do to the sons
>
> *ISRAÉL KAKA TA OCHURÓMATA AUTÓN EXAPOSTELEIS*
> of Israel bad the   fortresses   of them   send out
>
> *EN PURI KAI TOUS **EKLEKTOUS** AUTÓN EN RHOMPHAIA*
> in fire and the   choice   of them in broadsword
>
> *APOKTENEIS KAI TA NÉPIA AUTÓN ENSEISEIS KAI TAS*
>   kill   and the infants of them shall dash and the
>
> *EN GASTRI ECHOUSAS AUTÓN ANARRÉXEIS*
> in womb   having   of them   shall gut

engLXX

> And Azael said, "Why does my lord weep?" And he said,
> "Because I know all the evil that thou wilt do to the children
> of Israel: thou wilt utterly destroy their strong holds with fire,
> and thou wilt slay their choice men with the sword, and thou
> wilt dash their infants *against the ground*, and their women
> with child thou wilt rip up."

---

2 Kings 19:23 MIBCHOR (7-23)

> **By your messengers you have reproached the Lord, and
> said: "By the multitude of my chariots I have come up to the
> height of the mountains, to the limits of Lebanon; I will cut
> down its tall cedars *and* its choice cypress trees; I will enter
> the extremity of its borders, *to* its fruitful forest.**

LXX 4 Kings 19:23

> *EN CHEIRI AGGELÓN SOU ÓNEIDISAS KURION KAI*
> in hand | of you reproach   Lord   and
>   of messengers
>
> *EIPAS EN TÓ PLÉTHEI TÓN HARMATÓN MOU EGÓ*
> said   in the multitude of the chariots   of me I

ANABÉSOMAI EIS HUPSOS OREÓN MÉROUS TOU
ascend   into height of mountains sides   of the

LIBANOU KAI EKOPSA TO MEGETHOS TÉS KEDROU
Lebanon   and   cut   the   great   of the cedar

*AUTOU TA **EKLEKTA** KUPARISSÓN AUTOU KAI*
of him the choice   cypresses   of him and

ÉLTHON EIS MESON DRUMOU KAI KARMÉLOU
come   into midst   of wood and of Carmel

engLXX

> By thy messengers thou hast reproached the Lord, and hast said, I will go up with the multitude of my chariots, to the height of the mountains, to the sides of Libanus, and I have cut down the height of his cedar, and his choice cypresses; and I have come into the midst of the forest and of Carmel.

Ezra 5:8 GELAL (8-23)

> **Let it be known to the king that we went into the province of Judea, to the temple of the great God, which is being built with heavy stones, and timber is being laid in the walls; and this work goes on diligently and prospers in their hands.**

LXX Ezra 5:7

. . . *DAREÓ TÓ BASILEI EIRÉNÉ PASA*
Darius to the king   peace   all

5:8

GNÓSTON ESTÓ TÓ BASILEI HOTI EPOREUTHÉMEN EIS
known   be to the king since we conveyed   into

TÉN IOUDAIAN CHÓRAN EIS OIKON TOU THEOU TOU
the   Judea   area into house of the God of the

MEGALOU KAI AUTOS OIKODOMEITAI LITHOIS
Great   and   he   built   stones

***EKLEKTOIS** KAI XULA ENTITHETAI EN TOIS*
choice   and timber inserted   in to the

TOICHOIS KAI TO ERGON EKEINO EPIDEXION GINETAI
walls   and the   work   that   fittingly   being

KAI EUODOUTAI EN TAIS CHERSIN AUTÓN
and   prospers   in   the   hands   of them

engLXX

Be it known to the king, that we went into the land of Judea, to the house of the great God; and it is building with choice stones, and they are laying timbers in the walls, and that work is prospering, and goes on favourably in their hands.

Psalm 141:4 MANAMMIM (9-23)

Do not incline my heart to any evil thing, to practice wicked works with men who work iniquity; and do not let me eat of their delicacies.

LXX Psalm 140:4

MÉ EKKLINÉS TÉN KARDIAN MOU EIS LOGOUS
not turn aside   the   heart   of me to   words

PONÉRIAS TOU PROPHASIZESTHAI PROPHASEIS EN
evil   of the   to allege   excuse   in

HAMARTIAIS SUN ANTHRÓPOIS ERGAZOMENOIS TÉN
sins   with   men   working   the

ANOMIAN KAI OU MÉ SUNDOIASÓ META TÓN
lawlessness and in no wise   gather   with   the

EKLEKTÓN *AUTÓN*
choice   of them

engLXX

Incline not my heart to evil things, to employ pretexts for sins, with men who work iniquity: and let me not unite with their choice ones.

Proverbs 8:19 BACHAR (10-23)

My fruit *is* better than gold, yes, than fine gold, and my revenue than **choice** silver.

LXX

BELTION EME KARPIZESTHAI HUPER CHRUSION KAI
  best   my   enjoy fruit   over   gold   and

LITHON TIMION TA DE EMA GENNÉMATA KREISSÓ
  stones precious the but my   produce   better

*ARGURIOU **EKLEKTOU***
  of silver   of choice

engLXX

It is better to have my fruit than to have gold and precious stones; and my produce is better than choice silver.

Proverbs 12:24 CHARUTS (11-23)

The hand of the **diligent** will rule, but the slothful will be put to forced labor.

LXX

*CHEIR **EKLEKTÓN** KRATÉSEI EUCHERÓS DOLIOI DE*
  hand   of choice shall prevail easily   deceitful but

ESONTAI EN PRONOMÉ
  shall be in   captivity

engLXX

The hand of chosen men shall easily obtain rule; but the deceitful shall be for a prey.

Song of Solomon 6:9 BAR (12-23)

My dove, my perfect one, is the only one, the only one of her mother, the **favorite** of the one who bore her. The daughters saw her and called her blessed, the queens and the concubines, and they praised her.

My dove, my undefiled is *but* one; she is the *only* one of her mother, she *is* the **choice** one of her that bare her. The daughters saw her, and blessed her; *yea*, the queens and the concubines, and they praised her.   *KJV*

But my dove, my perfect one, is unique: she is her mother's only *daughter*; she is the **pure** *child* of the one who bore her. The maidens saw her and called her blessed, the queens and the concubines *also*, and they praised her, *saying*,   *NASB*

LXX 6:8

MIA ESTI PERISTERA MOU TELEIA MOU MIA ESTI TÉ
　my　is　　dove　　of me　perfect　of me　my　is　to the

*MÉTRI AUTÉS **EKLEKTÉ** ESTI TÉ TEKOUSÉ AUTÉN*
mother of her　　choice　　is　the　engender　her

EIDOSAN AUTÉN THUGATERES KAI MAKARIOUSIN
　saw　　her　　daughters　　and　　bless

AUTÉN BASILISSAI KAI GE PALLAKAI AINESOUSIN
　her　　queens　　and indeed concubines shall praise

AUTÉN
　her

engLXX

My dove, my perfect one is one; she is the *only* one of her mother; she is the choice of her that bore her. The daughters saw her, and the queens will pronounce her blessed, yea, and the concubines, and they will praise her.

Isaiah 22:8 NESHEQ (13-23)

He removed the protection of Judah. You looked in that day to the **armor** of the House of the Forest;

LXX

> *KAI ANAKALUPSOUSI TAS PULAS IOUDA KAI*
> and   shall uncover   the   gates   of Juda   and
>
> *EMBLEPSONTAI TÉ HÉMERA EKEINÉ EIS TOUS*
> shall look   in the   day   that   into   the
>
> ***EKLEKTOUS*** *OIKOUS TÉS POLEÓS*
> choice   houses of the   city

engLXX

> And they shall uncover the gates of Juda, and they shall look
> in that day on the choice houses of the city.

Isaiah 28:16 BOCHAN (14-23)

> Therefore thus says the Lord GOD:
> "Behold, I lay in Zion a stone for a foundation, a **tried**
> stone, a precious cornerstone, a sure foundation; whoever
> believes will not act hastily.

LXX

> *DIATOUTO HOUTÓ LEGEI KURIOS KURIOS IDOU EGÓ*
> therefore   thus   says   Lord   Lord   look   I
>
> *EMBALLÓ EIS TA THEMELIA SIÓN LITHON POLUTELÉ*
> put   into the foundations Zion   stone   costly
>
> ***EKLEKTON*** *AKROGÓNIAION ENTIMON EIS TA*
> choice   cornering   valuable   into the
>
> *THEMELIA AUTÉS KAI HO PISTEUÓN OU MÉ*
> foundations of her and the believing in no wise
>
> *KATAISCHUNTHÉ*
> dishonour

engLXX

> Therefore thus saith the Lord, even the Lord, Behold, I lay for
> the foundations of Sion a costly stone, a choice, a corner-stone,
> a precious stone, for its foundations; and he that believes on

him shall by no means be ashamed.

Isaiah 54:12 CHEPHETS (15-23)

I will make your pinnacles of rubies, your gates of crystal, and all your walls of precious stones.

LXX

KAI THÉSÓ TAS EPALXEIS SOU IASPIN KAI TAS PULAS
and will set the battlements of you jasper and the gates

SOU LITHOUS KRUSTALLOU KAI TON PERIBOLON SOU
of you stones crystal and the enclosure of you

*LITHOUS **EKLEKTOUS***
  stones choice

engLXX

and I will make thy buttresses jasper, and thy gates crystal, and thy border precious stones.

Jeremiah 3:19 CHEMDAH/CHAMUDOTH (16-23)

"But I said: 'How can I put you among the children and give you a **pleasant** land, a beautiful heritage of the hosts of nations?' And I said: 'You shall call Me, "My Father," and not turn away from Me.'

LXX

KAI EGÓ EIPA GENOITO KURIE HOTI TAXÓ SE EIS
 and I said it be Lord since | you into
                          shall arrange

*TEKNA KAI DÓSÓ SOI GÉN **EKLEKTÉN** KLÉRONOMIAN*
children and | to you land choice inheritance
       shall give

THEOU PANTOKRATOROS ETHNÓN KAI EIPA PATERA
 of God Almighty of nations and said Father

KALESETE ME KAI AP EMOU OUK APOSTRAPHÉSESTHE
 ye call me and from me not ye turn

engLXX
> And I said, So be it, Lord, for *thou saidst* I will set thee among children, and will give thee a choice land, the inheritance of the Almighty God of the Gentiles: and I said, Ye shall call me Father; and ye shall not turn away from me.

Jeremiah 10:17 MATSOR (17-23)

> Gather up your wares from the land, O inhabitant of the **fortress**!

> Gather from the land thy merchandise, O dweller in the **bulwark**,   *YLT*

LXX
> *SUNÉGAGEN EXÓTHEN TÉN HUPOSTASIN SOU*
> gather   from without the   substance of you
>
> *KATOIKOUSAN EN **EKLEKTOIS***
> dwelling   in   choice

engLXX
> He has gathered thy substance from without that lodged in choice *vessels*.

Ezekiel 7:20 TSEBI (18-23)

> 'As for the **beauty** of his ornaments, He set it in majesty; but they made from it the images of their abominations *and* their detestable things; therefore I have made it like refuse to them.

LXX
> ***EKLEKTA** KOSMOU EIS HUPERÉPHANIAN ETHENTO*
> choice   decoration into   arrogance   set
>
> *AUTA KAI EIKONAS TÓN BDELUGMATÓN AUTÓN*
> them and   images of the abominations   of them
>
> *EPOIÉSAN EX AUTÓN HENEKEN TOUTOU DEDÓKA*
> made out of them on account of this   gave

AUTA AUTOIS EIS AKATHARSIAN
them to them into   uncleanness

engLXX

As *for* their choice ornaments, they employed them for pride, and they made of them images of their abominations: therefore have I made them uncleanness to them.

Ezekiel 17:22 TSAMMERETH (19-23)

Thus says the Lord GOD: "I will take also *one* of the **highest branches** of the high cedar and set *it* out. I will crop off from the topmost of its young twigs a tender one, and will plant *it* on a high and prominent mountain.

LXX

DIOTI TADE LEGEI KURIOS KAI LÉPSOMAI EGÓ EK TÓN
since thus says Lord and take   I out of the

EKLEKTÓN TÉS KEDROU EK KORUPHÉS KARDIAS
choice   of the cedar out of crown   of hearts

AUTÓN APOKNIÓ KAI KATAPHUTEUSÓ EGÓ
of them pluck and   plant   I

EP OROS HUPSÉLON
upon mountain high

engLXX

For thus saith the Lord; I will even take of the choice *branches* of the cedar from the top *thereof*, I will crop off their hearts, and I will plant it on a high mountain:

Ezekiel 19:12 PERI (20-23)

But she was plucked up in fury, she was cast down to the ground, and the east wind dried her **fruit**. Her strong branches were broken and withered; the fire consumed them.

LXX

KAI KATEKLASTHÉ EN THUMÓ EPI GÉN ERRHIPHÉ KAI
and broken down in rage upon ground tossed and

*ANEMOS HO KAUSÓN EXÉRANE TA **EKLEKTA** AUTÉS*
wind the hot dried up the choice of her

EXEDIKÉTHÉSAN KAI EXÉRANTHÉ HÉ RHABDOS
were punished and were dried the rods

ISCHUOS AUTÉS PUR ANÉLÓSEN AUTÉN
of strength of her fire consumed her

engLXX

But she was broken down in wrath, she was cast upon the ground, and the east wind dried up her choice *branches*: vengeance came upon them, and the rod of her strength was withered; fire consumed it.

Ezekiel 27:20 CHOPHESH (21-23)

Dedan *was* your merchant in **saddlecloths** for riding.

Dedan *was* thy merchant in **precious** clothes for chariots.

KJV

LXX

*DAIDAN EMPOROI SOU META KTÉNÓN **EKLEKTÓN***
Daidan merchants of you with livestock choice

EIS HARMATA
to chariots

engLXX

The people of Dædan were thy merchants, with choice cattle for chariots.

Ezekiel 27:24 BEROMIM (22-23)

These *were* your merchants in choice items—in purple clothes, in embroidered garments, in chests of **multicolored**

apparel, in strong twined cords, which were in your marketplace.

LXX

PHERONTES EMPORIAN HUAKINTHON KAI THÉSAUROUS
   bring   commerce   of blue   and   treasures

EKLEKTOUS *DEDEMENOUS SCHOINIOIS KAI*
   choice   bound   with chords and

KUPARISSINA
   cypress

engLXX

bringing *for* merchandise blue, and choice stores bound with cords, and cypress wood.

Amos 5:11 MASETH (23-23)

Therefore, because you tread down the poor and take grain **taxes** from him, though you have built houses of hewn stone, yet you shall not dwell in them; you have planted pleasant vineyards, but you shall not drink wine from them. Forasmuch therefore as your treading *is* upon the poor, and ye take from him **burdens** of wheat: ye have built houses of hewn stone, but ye shall not dwell in them; ye have planted pleasant vineyards, but ye shall not drink wine of them.

KJV

LXX

DIATOUTO ANTH HÓN KATEKONDULIZON PTÓCHOUS
   therefore for the sake of whom ye struck   poor

KAI DÓRA **EKLEKTA** *EDEXASTHE PAR AUTÓN OIKOUS*
   and gifts   choice   ye took   from them   houses

XESTOUS ÓKODOMÉSATE KAI OU MÉ KATOIKÉSÉTE
   planed   ye built   and in no wise ye shall dwell

EN AUTOIS AMPELÓNAS EPITHUMÉTOUS

in   them   vineyards   desirable

EPHUTEUSATE KAI OU MÉ PIÉTE TON OINON AUTÓN
ye shall plant   and in no wise ye drink the wine   of them

engLXX
> Therefore because they have smitten the poor with their fists, and ye have received of them choice gifts; ye have built polished houses, but ye shall not dwell in them; ye have planted desirable vineyards, but ye shall not drink the wine of them.

We just saw in order of appearance the Hebrew words MIBCHAR (**choicest**), BARI (**fat**), DEROR (**liquid/pure** myrrh KJV), BE-CHURIM/BECHUROTH (**choice men/young men** KJV), BARAR (**pure + pure**), BACHUR (**young men**), MIBCHOR (**choice**), GELAL (**heavy** stones), MANAMMIM (**delicacies**), BACHAR (**choice** silver), CHARUTS (**diligent**), BAR (**favourite/choice** KJV/**pure** *child* NASB), NESHEQ (**armor** of the House), BOCHAN (**tried** stone), CHEPHETS (**precious** stones), CHEMDAH/CHAMUDOTH (**pleasant** land), MATSOR (**fortress/bulwark** YLT), TSEBI (**beauty**), TSAMMERETH (**highest branches**), PERI (**fruit**), CHOPHESH (**saddlecloths/precious** clothes KJV), BEROMIM (**multicolored apparel**), MASETH (**taxes/burdens** of wheat KJV).

We saw that every one of these 23 Heb. words were translated by the one Greek word *EKLEKTOS* in the LXX.

And none of these here give an indication of "chosen/selected/elect".

So, every Hebrew word translated by *EKLEKTOS* in the LXX has been translated into English with a top quality meaning. This is one example each.

What do you think?

With Jesus having read the LXX and seeing all those uses of *EKLEKTOS* there, what did He mean by saying:

For many are called, but few *EKLEKTOS*.   *Matthew 22:14*

For many are called, but few *have* mettle.   *Matthew 22:14 JM*

45

More than just one example

But, that is not all there is to it. Some of these Hebrew words are like BACHIR, only translated by *EKLEKTOS*, some have two meanings and, some have more occasions to show the top quality emphasis. Let's unpack some more.

Only translated by *EKLEKTOS*

Just like the Hebrew word BACHIR, there are another 4 Hebrew words which are also only translated by *EKLEKTOS*, but unlike BACHIR, these 4 occur only once:

BEROMIM (**multicolored apparel**), BOCHAN (**tried** stone), CHOPHESH (**saddlecloths/precious** clothes KJV) and, MANAMMIM (**delicacies**). Since each of these occur only once as translated by *EKLEKTOS*, they are shown in full in the preceding chapter.

Hebrew words with top quality meaning

All the remaining Hebrew words, undisputed in their use as a top quality meaning (and like the 4 Hebrew words above, also now in alphabetical order):

BAR

"**favorite/choice** *one* KJV/**pure** *child* NASB"

– to clean, to purify – from BARAR

As well as Song of Solomon 6:9 (1-2) the other place where it is translated by *EKLEKTOS* in the LXX:

Song of Solomon 6:10 "**clear/pure** NASB/**bright** as the sun NIV"

Song of Solomon 6:10 BAR (2-2)

Who is she *who* looks forth as the morning, fair as the moon, **clear** as the sun, awesome as *an army* with banners?

'Who is this that grows like the dawn, as beautiful as the

full moon, as **pure** as the sun, as awesome as an army
with banners?'   *NASB*

Who is this that appears like the dawn, fair as the moon,
bright as the sun, majestic as the stars in procession?   *NIV*

LXX 6:9

TIS AUTÉ HÉ EKKUPTOUSA HÓSEI ORTHROS KALÉ HÓS
who she the   looking out   as   dawn   fair   as

*SELÉNÉ **EKLEKTÉ** HÓS* **HO HÉLIOS THAMBOS**
moon   choice   as   the   sun   amazing

HÓS TETAGMENAI
as   set in array [soldiers]

engLXX

Who is this that looks forth as the morning, fair as the moon,
choice as the sun, terrible as *armies* set in array?

Of the 7 instances of BAR in the LXX **2** are given as **EKLEKTOS**, 2 are
KATHAROS (clean, pure), 1 is *AMEMPTOS* (blameless), 1 is *EUTHUS*
(straight, direct) and, 1 is *TÉLAUGÉS* *not in the NT* (far shining).

All the references for BAR are:
Job 11:4; Psalm 19:8; Psalm 24:4; Psalm 73:1; Proverbs 14:4; **Song of
Songs 6:9**; **Song of Songs 6:10**

BARI
"**fat**" – full fleshed, firm

As well as Genesis 41:2 (1-9) the other places where it is translated
by *EKLEKTOS* in the LXX:

Genesis 41:4	"**fat**"
Genesis 41:5	"**plump**"
Genesis 41:7	"**plump**"
Genesis 41:18	"**fat**"
Genesis 41:20	"**fat**"
1 Kings 4:23	"**fatted** oxen"

Habakkuk 1:16   "food **plentious**"
Zechariah 11:16   "**fat**"

Genesis 41:4 BARI (2-9)

And the ugly and gaunt cows ate up the seven fine looking and fat cows. So Pharaoh awoke.

LXX

KAI KATEPHAGON HAI HEPTA BOES HAI AISCHRAI KAI
 and   ate   the   seven   oxen the reproachful and

LEPTAI TAIS SARXI TAS HEPTA BOAS TAS KALAS
 thin with the flesh the seven oxen the   fair

*TÓ EIDEI KAI TAS **EKLEKTAS** TAIS SARXI ÉGERTHÉ*
to the sight and the   choice   with the flesh   roused

DE PHARAÓ
but Pharaoh

engLXX

And the seven ill-favoured and lean cows devoured the seven
well-favoured and choice-fleshed cows; and Pharao awoke.

Genesis 41:5 BARI (3-9)

He slept and dreamed a second time; and suddenly seven heads of grain came up on one stalk, plump and good.

LXX

KAI ENUPNIASTHÉ TO DEUTERON KAI IDOU HEPTA
 and   dreamed   the   second   and look seven

STACHUES ANEBAINON EN TÓ PUTHMENI HENI
  ears   came up   in the   stem   one

***EKLEKTOI** KAI KALOI*
 choice   and good

engLXX

And he dreamed again. And, behold, seven ears came up on

one stalk, choice and good.

Genesis 41:7 BARI (4-9)

And the seven thin heads devoured the seven plump and full heads. So Pharaoh awoke, and indeed, *it was* a dream.

LXX

KAI KATEPION HOI HEPTA STACHUES HOI LEPTOI KAI
and consumed the seven   ears   the thin and

ANEMOPHTHOROI TOUS HEPTA STACHUAS TOUS
wind destroyed the seven ears the

EKLEKTOUS *KAI TOUS PLÉREIS ÉGERTHÉ DE*
choice and the full arose but

PHARAÓ KAI ÉN ENUPNION
Pharaoh and was dream

engLXX

And the seven thin ears and blasted with the wind devoured the seven choice and full ears; and Pharao awoke, and it was a dream.

Genesis 41:18 BARI (5-9)

Suddenly seven cows came up out of the river, fine looking and fat; and they fed in the meadow.

LXX

KAI HÓSPER EK TOU POTAMOU ANEBAINON HEPTA
and even as out of the river came up seven

BOES KALAI TÓ EIDEI KAI **EKLEKTAI** *TAIS SARXI*
oxen fair to the sight and choice with the flesh

KAI ENEMONTO EN TÓ AXEI
and graze in the sedge

engLXX

and there came up as it were out of the river, seven cows

well-favoured and choice-fleshed, and they fed on the sedge.

Genesis 41:20 BARI (6-9)

And the gaunt and ugly cows ate up the first seven, the fat cows.

LXX

KAI KATEPHAGON HAI HEPTA BOES HAI AISCHRAI KAI
and   ate up   the seven oxen the reproachful and

LEPTAI TAS HEPTA BOAS TAS PRÓTAS TAS KALAS
 thin   the seven oxen the   first   the   fair

*KAI TAS **EKLEKTAS***
 and the   choice

engLXX

And the seven ill-favoured and thin cows ate up the seven first good and choice cows.

---

1 Kings 4:23 BARI (7-9)

ten fatted oxen, twenty oxen from the pastures, and one hundred sheep, besides deer, gazelles, roebucks, and fatted fowl.

LXX 3 Kings 4:23

*KAI DEKA MOSCHOI **EKLEKTOI** KAI EIKOSI BOES*
 and ten   calves   choice   and twenty oxen

NOMADES KAI HEKATON PROBATA EKTOS ELAPHÓN
 grazing and hundred   sheep   outside of stags

KAI DORKADÓN EKLEKTÓN[1] SITEUTA
 and   does   choice   fatted

[1]This second *EKLEKTOS* does not directly translate a Hebrew word

(See DEiTB).

engLXX

and ten choice calves, and twenty pastured oxen, and a hundred sheep, besides stags, and choice fatted does.

Habakkuk 1:16 BARI (8-9)

Therefore they sacrifice to their net, and burn incense to their dragnet; because by them their share *is* sumptuous and their food **plentious**.

LXX

HENEKEN TOUTOU THUSEI TÉ SAGÉNÉ AUTOU KAI
therefore   of this   sacrifice the dragnet of him and

THUMIASEI TÓ AMPHIBLÉSTRÓ AUTOU HOTI EN
burn incense to the casting net   of him since in

AUTOIS ELIPANE MERIDA AUTOU KAI TA BRÓMATA
them   fat   portion of him and the food

AUTOU EKLEKTA
of him   choice

engLXX
Therefore will he sacrifice to his drag, and burn incense to his casting-net, because by them he has made his portion fat, and his meats choice.

Zechariah 11:16 BARI (9-9)

For indeed I will raise up a shepherd in the land *who* will not care for those who are cut off, nor seek the young, nor heal those that are broken, nor feed those that still stand. But he will eat the flesh of the **fat** and tear their hooves in pieces.

LXX

DIOTI IDOU EGÓ EXEGEIRÓ POIMENA EPI TÉN GÉN TO
for   look I   raise   shepherd over the land the

EKLIMPANON OU MÉ EPISKEPSÉTAI KAI TO
omit   in no wise   look after   and the

ESKORPISMENON OU MÉ ZÉTÉSÉ KAI TO
dispersed   in no wise seek   and the

SUNTETRIMMENON OU MÉ IASÉTAI KAI TO
broken   in no wise heal   and the

HOLOKLÉRON OU MÉ KATEUTHUNÉ KAI TA KREA TÓN
  whole   in no wise   conduct   and the meat of the

EKLEKTÓN *KATAPHAGETAI KAI TOUS ASTRAGALOUS*
  choice   devour   and the   vertebrae

AUTÓN EKSTREPSEI
of them   twist

engLXX

For, behold, I *will* raise up a shepherd against the land: he shall not visit that which is perishing, and he shall not seek that which is scattered, and he shall not heal that which is bruised, nor guide that which is whole: but he shall devour the flesh of the choice ones, and shall dislocate the joints *of their necks.*

Of the 13 instances of BARI in the LXX **9** are given as **EKLEKTOS**, 1 is *ASTEIOS* (handsome), 1 is *ISCHUROS* (strong, mighty), 1 is *PACHUS* *not in the NT* (stout) and, 1 is *STEREÓMA* (firm).

All the references for BARI are:
Genesis 41:2; **Genesis 41:4**; **Genesis 41:5**; **Genesis 41:7**; **Genesis 41:18**; **Genesis 41:20**; Judges 3:17; **1 Kings 4:23**; Psalm 73:4; Ezekiel 34:3; Daniel 1:15; **Habakkuk 1:16**; **Zechariah 11:16**

BECHURIM/BECHUROTH
"**choice men/young men** KJV" – young men, youth

This is only translated by *EKLEKTOS* in Numbers 11:28, as shown in the preceding chapter.

Of the 3 instances of BECHURIM/BECHUROTH in the LXX **1** is given as **EKLEKTO**S and, 2 are *NEOTÉS* (youth).

All the references for BECHURIM/BECHUROTH are:
Numbers 11:28; Ecclesiastes 11:9; Ecclesiastes 12:1

CHARUTS
"**diligent**" – being diligent, gold

This is only translated by *EKLEKTOS* in Proverbs 12:24, as shown in the preceding chapter.

Of the 18 instances of CHARUTS in the LXX **1** is given as **EKLEKTOS**, 6 are *CHRUSION* (gold), 2 are *ANDREIOS* *not in the NT* (manly, vigorous), 2 are *DIKÉ* (judgment, vengeance), 1 is *CHRUSOS* (gold), one is *KATHAROS* (pure, honest), 1 is *PRIÓN* *not in the NT* (saw [the tool]), one is *SKLÉROTÉS* (hard, rigid), one is *TEICHOS* (wall), one is *TROCHOS* (wheel) and, 1 is not translated.

All the references for CHARUTS are:
Job 41:30; Psalm 68:13; Proverbs 3:14; Proverbs 8:10; Proverbs 8:19; Proverbs 10:4; **Proverbs 12:24**; Proverbs 12:27; Proverbs 13:4; Proverbs 16:16; Proverbs 21:5; Isaiah 28:27; Isaiah 41:15; Daniel 9:25; Joel 3:14a; Joel 3:14b; Amos 1:3; Zechariah 1:3

CHEMDAH/CHAMUDOTH
"**pleasant** land" – desirable, beautiful, precious

As well as Jeremiah 3:19 (1-4) the other places where it is translated by *EKLEKTOS* in the LXX:

Jeremiah 25:34	"**precious** vessel"
Haggai 2:7	"**Desire** of All Nations"
Zechariah 7:14	"**pleasant** land"

Jeremiah 25:34 CHEMDAH/CHAMUDOTH (2-4)

"**Wail, shepherds, and cry! Roll about *in the ashes*, you leaders of the flock! For the days of your slaughter and your dispersions are fulfilled; you shall fall like a precious vessel.**

LXX 32:34
ALALAXATE POIMENES KAI KEKRAXATE KAI
   shout   shepherds and   cry out   and

KOPTESTHE HOI KRIOI TÓN PROBATÓN
  smite   the chest   the (rams of the) sheep
HOTI EPLÉRÓTHÉSAN HAI HÉMERAI HUMÓN EIS
  since   filled   the   days   of you   into

SPHAGÉN KAI PESEISTHE HÓSPER HOI KRIOI
  slaughter and   ye fall   even as   the   rams

*HOI **EKLEKTOI***
  the   choice

engLXX

Howl, ye shepherds, and cry; and lament, ye rams of the flock:
for your days have been completed for slaughter, and ye shall
fall as the choice rams.

Haggai 2:7 CHEMDAH/CHAMUDOTH (3-4)

**and I will shake all nations, and they shall come to the
Desire of All Nations, and I will fill this temple with glory,'
says the LORD of hosts.**

LXX 2:8

KAI SUSSEISÓ PANTA TA ETHNÉ KAI HÉXEI
and I shall shake all   the nations and shall come

*TA **EKLEKTA** PANTÓN TÓN ETHNÓN KAI PLÉSÓ*
 the   choice   of all of the nations and I shall fill
TON OIKON TOUTON DOXÉS LEGEI KURIOS PANTOKRATÓR
 the house   this   with glory says Lord   Almighty

engLXX

and I will shake all nations, and the choice portions of all the
nations shall come: and I will fill this house with glory, saith
the Lord Almighty.

Zechariah 7:14 CHEMDAH/CHAMUDOTH (4-4)

"But I scattered them with a whirlwind among all the na-

tions which they had not known. Thus the land became desolate after them, so that no one passed through or returned;
for they made the **pleasant** land desolate."

LXX

KAI EKBALÓ AUTOUS EIS PANTA TA ETHNÉ HA OUK
and cast out   them   into   all   the nations which not

EGNÓSAN KAI HÉ GÉ APHANISTHÉSETAI KATOPISTHEN
  knew   and the land   destroy   behind

AUTÓN EK DIODEUONTOS KAI EX ANASTREPHONTOS
of them out of travel through and out of   returning

*KAI ETAXAN GÉN **EKLEKTÉN** EIS APHANISMON*
 and   set   land   choice   into destruction

engLXX

And I will cast them out among all the nations, whom they
know not; and the land behind them shall be made utterly
destitute of any going through or returning: yea they have
made the choice land a desolation.

Of the 25 instances of CHEMDAH/CHAMUDOTH in the LXX **4**
are given as **EKLEKTOS**, 11 are *EPITHUMÉTOS* *not in the NT*
(desirable), 5 are *EPITHUMIA* (desire, yearning), 1 is *EPAINOS*
(praise), 1 is *EPITHUMÉMA* *not in the NT* (object of desire),
1 is *HÓRAIOS* (beautiful), 1 is *KALOS* (good) and, 1 is *KALLOS* *not
in the NT* (beauty).

All the references for CHEMDAH/CHAMUDOTH are:
Genesis 27:15; 1 Samuel 9:20; 2 Chronicles 20:25; 2Chronicles 21:20;
2Chronicles 32:27; 2Ch. 36:10; Ezra 8:27; Psalm 106:24; Isaiah 2:16;
Jeremiah 3:19; Jeremiah 12:10; **Jeremiah 25:34**; Ezekiel 26:12;
Daniel 9:23; Daniel 10:3; Daniel 10:11; Daniel 10:19; Daniel 11:8;
Daniel 11:37; Daniel 11:38; Daniel 11:43; Hosea 13:15; Nahum 2:9;
Haggai 2:7; **Zechariah 7:14**

CHEPHETS
"**pleasant** stones" – desirable, delightful, gladly

This is only translated by *EKLEKTOS* in Isaiah 54:12, as shown in the preceding chapter.

Of the 39 instances of CHEPHETS in the LXX **1** is given as **EKLEKTOS**, 19 are *THELÉMA* (desire, will), 4 are *PRAGMA* (deed, act), 3 are *CHREIA* (need), 2 are *AXIOS* (worthy), 2 are *THELÉTOS* *not in the NT* (wished for, desired), 1 is *ACHRÉSTOS* (unprofitable, useless), 1 is *BOULOMAI* (to will, wish), 1 is *BOULEU-Ó/OMAI* (take counsel), 1 is *ERGON* (work), 1 is *EUCHRÉSTOS* (useful, serviceable), 1 is *MELÓ* (to care), 1 is *THELÓ* (to be willing) and, 1 is not translated.

All the references for CHEPHETS are:
1Samuel 15:22; 1Samuel 18:25; 2Samuel 23:5; 1Kings 5:8; 1Kings 5:9; 1Kings 5:10; 1Kings 9:11; 1Kings 10:13; 2 Chronicles 9:12; Job 21:21; Job 22:3; Job 31:16; Psalm 1:2; Psalm 16:3; Psalm 107:30; Psalm 111:2; Proverbs 3:15; Proverbs 8:11; Proverbs 31:13; Ecclesiastes 3:1; Ecclesiastes 3:17; Ecclesiastes 5:4; Ecclesiastes 5:8; Ecclesiastes 8:6; Ecclesiastes 12:1; Ecclesiastes 12:10; Isaiah 44:28; Isaiah 46:10; Isaiah 48:14; Isaiah 53:10; **Isaiah 54:12**; Isaiah 58:3; Isaiah 58:13a; Isaiah 58:13b; Jeremiah 22:28; Jeremiah 48:38; Hosea 8:8; Malachi 1:10; Malachi 3:12

DEROR
"**liquid/pure** myrrh KJV" – liberty, pure, swallow

This is only translated by *EKLEKTOS* in Exodus 30:23, as shown in the preceding chapter.

Of the 10 instances of DEROR in the LXX **1** is given as **EKLEKTOS**, 7 are *APHESIS* (release), 1 is *STROUTHOS* *not in the NT* (sparrow) and, 1 is *TRUGÓN* (turtle-dove).

All the references for DEROR are:
Exodus 30:23; Leviticus 25:10; Psalm 84:3; Proverbs 26:2; Isaiah 61:1;

Jeremiah 34:8; Jeremiah 34:15; Jeremiah 34:17a; Jeremiah 34:17b; Ezekiel 46:17

GELAL
"**heavy** stones" – great (i.e. massive)

This is only translated by *EKLEKTOS* in Ezra 5:8, as shown in the preceding chapter.

Of the 2 instances of GELAL in the LXX **1** is given as ***EKLEKTOS*** and, 1 is *KRATAIOS* (mighty, great, strong).

All the references for GELAL are:
Ezra 5:8; Ezra 6:4

MASETH
"**burdens/taxes** of wheat KJV" – portions, burdens

This is only translated by *EKLEKTOS* in Amos 5:11, as shown in the preceding chapter.

Of the 15 instances of MASETH in the LXX **1** is given as ***EKLEKTOS***, 2 are *MERIS* (part, portion), 2 are *SUSSÉMON* (signal), 1 is *APHORISMOS* *not in the NT* (offering), 1 is *ARSIS* *not in the NT* (distilled, portion), 1 is *DÓRON* (gift, present), 1 is *EPARSIS* *not in the NT* (rising, swelling), 1 is *KRINÓ* (distinguish, judge), 1 is *LAMBANÓ* (to take, receive), 1 is *LÉMMA* *not in the NT* (argument), 1 is *SÉMEION* (mark, sign) and, 2 are not translated.

All the references for MASETH are:
Genesis 43:34a; Genesis 43:34b; Judges 20:38; Judges 20:40; 2 Samuel 11:8; 2 Chronicles 24:6; 2 Chronicles 24:9; Esther 2:18; Psalm 141:2; Jeremiah 6:1; Jeremiah 40:5; Lamentations 2:14; Ezekiel 20:40; **Amos 5:11**; Zephaniah 3:18

MATSOR
"**fortress/bulwark** YLT" – fortress, bulwarks, stronghold

This is only translated by *EKLEKTOS* in Jeremiah 10:17, as shown in the preceding chapter.

Of the 30 instances of MATSOR in the LXX **1** is given as ***EKLEKTOS***, 10 are *PERIOCHÉ* (surrounding siege), 3 are *SUGKLEISMOS* *not in the NT* (siege), 3 are *THLIPSIS* (pressure, affliction), 2 are *OCHUROS* *not in the NT* (strong), 2 are *SUNOCHÉ* (besiege), 1 is *CHARAKÓSIS* *not in the NT* (siege), 1 is *CHARAX* (siege stake), 1 is *DIÓRUX* *not in the NT* (canal, defence trench), 1 is *OCHURÓMA* (fortress), 1 is *PETRA* (rock), 1 is *SUGKLEIÓ* (shut, closed), 1 is *SUNAGÓGÉ* (gathered together), 1 is *TEICHÉRÉS* *not in the NT* (walled in) and, 1 is *TUROS* (Tyre).

All the references for MATSOR are:
Deuteronomy 20:19; Deuteronomy 20:20; Deuteronomy 28:53; Deuteronomy 28:55; Deuteronomy 28:57; 2 Kings 19:24; 2 Kings 24:10; 2 Kings 25:2; 2 Chronicles 8:5; 2 Chronicles 11:5; 2 Chronicles 32:10; Psalm 31:21; Psalm 60:9; Isaiah 19:6; Isaiah 37:25; **Jeremiah 10:17**; Jeremiah 19:9; Jeremiah 52:5; Ezekiel 4:2; Ezekiel 4:3; Ezekiel 4:7; Ezekiel 4:8; Ezekiel 5:2; Micah 5:1; Micah 7:12a; Micah 7:12b; Nahum 3:14; Habakkuk 2:1; Zechariah 9:3; Zechariah 12:2

MIBCHOR
"**choice** fir trees" – choice

This is only translated by *EKLEKTOS* in 2 Kings 19:23, as shown in the preceding chapter.

Of the 2 instances of MIBCHOR in the LXX **1** is given as ***EKLEKTOS*** and, 1 is *OCHUROS* *not in the NT* (secure, strong).

All the references for MIBCHOR are:
2 Kings 3:19; **2 Kings 19:23**

NESHEQ
"**armor** of the House" – armour, weapons

This is only translated by *EKLEKTOS* in Isaiah 22:8, as shown in the preceding chapter.

Of the 10 instances of NESHEQ in the LXX **1** is given as ***EKLEKTOS***, 3 are *HOPLON* (arm, weapon), 1 is *ISCHUS* (strength), 1 is *POLEMOS* (war, battle), 1 is *PURGOS* (tower), 1 is *SIDÉROS* (iron) and, 2 are not translated.

All the references for NESHEQ are:
1 Kings 10:25; 2 Kings 10:2; 2 Chronicles 9:24; Nehemiah 3:19; Job 20:24; Job 39:21; Psalm 140:7; **Isaiah 22:8**; Ezekiel 39:9; Ezekiel 39:10

PERI
"**fruit**" – fruit

As well as Ezekiel 19:12 (1-2) the other place where it is translated by *EKLEKTOS* in the LXX:
Ezekiel 19:14   "**fruit**"

Ezekiel 19:14 PERI (2-2)

> Fire has come out from a rod of her branches *and* devoured her **fruit**, so that she has no strong branch— a scepter for ruling."
> This *is* a lamentation, and has become a lamentation.

LXX

*KAI EXÉLTHE PUR EK RHABDOU **EKLEKTÓN** AUTÉS*
and ye come out fire out of   rod   choice   of her

KAI KATEPHAGEN AUTÉN KAI OUK ÉN EN AUTÉ
and   eat up   her   and not was in   she

RHABDOS ISCHUOS PHULÉ EIS PARABOLÉN THRÉNOU
   rod   strong kindred into   parable   of lament

ESTI KAI ESTAI EIS THRÉNON
  is   and shall be into lamentation

englXX

> And fire is gone out of a rod of her choice *boughs*, and has devoured her; and there was no rod of strength in her. Her race is become a parable of lamentation, and it shall be for a lamentation.

Of the 119 instances of PERI in the LXX **2** are given as **EKLEKTOS**, 82 are *KARPOS* (fruit), 10 are *GENNÉMA* (produce), 10 are *EKGONOS* (born of), 2 are *EKPHORION* *not in the NT* (increase of land), 2 are *KARPOPHOROS* (fruitful), 1 is *BOUKOLION* *not in the NT* (herd), 1 is *EULOGIA* (blessing), 1 is *KARPIZ-Ó/-OMAI* *not in the NT* (enjoy fruit of), 1 is *KARPIMOS* *not in the NT* (fruit bearing), 1 is *SPERMA* (seed), 1 is *TEKNON* (child) and, 5 are not translated.

All the references for PERI are:
Genesis 1:11a; Genesis 1:11b; Genesis 1:12; Genesis 1:29; Genesis 3:2; Genesis 3:3; Genesis 3:6; Genesis 4:3; Genesis 30:2; Exodus 10:15; Leviticus 19:23; Leviticus 19:24; Leviticus 19:25; Leviticus 23:40; Leviticus 25:19; Leviticus 26:4; Leviticus 26:20; Leviticus 27:30; Numbers 13:20; Numbers 13:26; Numbers 13:27; Deuteronomy 1:25; Deuteronomy 7:13a; Deuteronomy 7:13b; Deuteronomy 26:2; Deuteronomy 26:10; Deuteronomy 28:4a; Deuteronomy 28:4b; Deuteronomy 28:4c; Deuteronomy 28:11a; Deuteronomy 28:11b; Deuteronomy 28:11c; Deuteronomy 28:18a; Deuteronomy 28:18b; Deuteronomy 28:33; Deuteronomy 28:42; Deuteronomy 28:51a; Deuteronomy 28:51b; Deuteronomy 28:53; Deuteronomy 30:9a; Deuteronomy 30:9b; Deuteronomy 30:9c; 2 Kings 19:29; 2 Kings 19:30; Nehemiah 9:36; Nehemiah 10:35; Nehemiah 10:37; Psalm 1:3; Psalm 21:10; Psalm 58:11;Psalm 72:16; Psalm 104:13; Psalm 105:35; Psalm 107:34; Psalm 107:37; Psalm 127:3; Psalm 132:11; Psalm 148:9; Proverbs 1:31; Proverbs 8:19; Proverbs 11:30; Proverbs 12:14; Proverbs 13:2; Proverbs 18:20; Proverbs 18:21; Proverbs 27:18; Proverbs 31:16; Proverbs 31:31; Ecclesiastes 2:5; Song of Songs 2:3; Song of Songs 4:13; Song of Songs 4:16; Song of Songs 8:11; Song of Songs 8:12; Isaiah 3:10; Isaiah 4:2; Isaiah 10:12; Isaiah 13:18; Isaiah 14:29; Isaiah 27:9; Isaiah 37:30; Isaiah 37:31; Isaiah 65:21; Jeremiah 2:7; Jeremiah 6:19; Jeremiah 7:20;

Jeremiah 11:16; Jeremiah 12:2; Jeremiah 17:8; Jeremiah 17:10; Jeremiah 21:14; Jeremiah 29:5; Jeremiah 29:28; Jeremiah 32:19; Lamentations 2:20; Ezekiel 17:8; Ezekiel 17:9; Ezekiel 17:23; **Ezekiel 19:12**; **Ezekiel 19:14**; Ezekiel 25:4; Ezekiel 34:27; Ezekiel 36:8; Ezekiel 36:30; Ezekiel 47:12a; Ezekiel 47:12b; Hosea 9:16; Hosea 10:1a; Hosea 10:1b; Hosea 10:13; Hosea 14:8; Joel 2:22; Amos 2:9; Amos 6:12; Amos 9:14; Micah 6:7; Micah 7:13; Zechariah 8:12; Malachi 3:11

TSAMMERETH
"**highest branches**" – highest branch, top

This is only translated by *EKLEKTOS* in Ezekiel 17:22, as shown in the preceding chapter.

Of the 5 instances of TSAMMERETH in the LXX **1** is given as ***EKLEKTOS***, 3 are *ARCHÉ* (top, first) and, 1 is *EPILEKTOS* *not in the NT* (over, best): of the same word family as *EKLEKTOS* with much the same meaning (See also the later chapter *Other historical pointers*).

All the references for TSAMMERETH are:
Ezekiel 17:3; Ezekiel 31:14; Ezekiel 17:22; Ezekiel 31:3; Ezekiel 31:10

TSEBI
"**beauty**" – beauty, glory, roebuck

As well as Ezekiel 7:20 (1-2) the other place where it is translated by *EKLEKTOS* in the LXX:
Ezekiel 25:9   "**glory** of the country"

Ezekiel 25:9 TSEBI (2-2)

> **therefore, behold, I will clear the territory of Moab of cities, of the cities on its frontier, the glory of the country, Beth Jeshimoth, Baal Meon, and Kirjathaim.**

LXX
> *DIATOUTO IDOU EGÓ PARALUÓ TON ÓMON MÓAB*
> therefore   look   I   disable   the shoulder of Moab

*APO POLEÓN AKRÓTÉRIÓN AUTOU **EKLEKTÉN** GÉN*
from   cities   of borders   of him   choice   land

OIKON BETHASIMOUTH EPANÓ PÉGÉS POLEÓS
 house   of Bethasimuth   above   spring   of city

PARATHALASSIAS
  by sea

engLXX

Therefore, behold, I will weaken the shoulder of Moab from his frontier cities, *even* the choice land, the house of Bethasimuth above the fountain of the city, by the sea-side.

Of the 5 instances of TSEBI in the LXX **2** are given as ***EKLEKTOS***, 10 are *DORKAS* *not in the NT* (doe, type of deer); 3 are *DUNAMIS* (power, might), 2 are *DOXA* (glory), 2 are *ELPIS* (hope, expectation), 2 are *ENDOXOS* (honoured, gloried), 2 are *KÉRION* (honeycomb), 1 is *DORKADION* *not in the NT* (fawn, little gazelle), 1 is *DORKÓN* *not in the NT* (roe, buck), 1 is *EPILAMPÓ* *not in the NT* (to shine upon), 1 is *STÉLOÓ* *not in the NT* (stand still, set up stone), 1 is *SABAEIM* *not in the NT* (beauty, glory), 1 is *SABAEIN* *not in the NT* (beauty, glory), 1 is *SABEI* *not in the NT* (beauty, glory) and, 2 are not translated.

All the references for TSEBI are:
Deuteronomy 12:15; Deuteronomy 12:22; Deuteronomy 14:5; Deuteronomy 15:22; 2 Samuel 1:19; 2 Samuel 2:18; 1 Kings 4:23; 1 Chronicles 12:8; Proverbs 6:5; Song of Songs 2:7; Song of Songs 2:9; Song of Songs 2:17; Song of Songs 3:5; Song of Songs 8:14; Isaiah 4:2; Isaiah 13:14; Isaiah 13:19; Isaiah 23:9; Isaiah 24:16; Isaiah 28:1; Isaiah 28:4; Isaiah 28:5; Jeremiah 3:19; **Ezekiel 7:20**; Ezekiel 20:6; Ezekiel 20:15; **Ezekiel 25:9**; Ezekiel 26:20; Daniel 8:9; Daniel 11:16; Daniel 11:41; Daniel 11:45

So, as well as the list of meanings seen in the previous chapter as follows:

MIBCHAR (**choicest**), BARI (**fat**), DEROR (**liquid/pure** myrrh KJV), BECHURIM/BECHUROTH (**choice men/young men** KJV), BARAR (**pure** + **pure**), BACHUR (**young men**), MIBCHOR (**choice**), GELAL (**heavy** stones), MANAMMIM (**delicacies**), BACHAR (**choice** silver), CHARUTS (**diligent**), BAR (**favourite/choice** KJV/**pure** *child* NASB), NESHEQ (**armor** of the House), BOCHAN (**tried** stone), CHEPHETS (**precious** stones), CHEMDAH/CHAMUDOTH (**pleasant** land), MATSOR (**fortress/bulwark** YLT), TSEBI (**beauty**), TSAMMERETH (**highest branches**), PERI (**fruit**), CHOPHESH (**saddlecloths/precious** clothes KJV), BEROMIM (**multicolored apparel**), MASETH (**taxes/burdens** of wheat KJV).

Except for four Hebrew words which I have reserved for the next chapter to be looked at, we now have the following English words to add to those from the above Hebrew words: I have shared here in this chapter all the Hebrew words with no appearance of doubt as to the meaning of top quality.

So, added are:
BAR ("**clear/pure** NASB/**bright** as the sun NIV"), BARI ("**fatted** oxen", "food **plentious**", "**plump**" two times &, "**fat**" a further 4 times), CHEMDAH/CHAMUDOTH ("**precious** vessel", "**Desire** of All Nations", "**pleasant** land"), PERI ("**fruit**" 1 more time), TSEBI ("**glory** of the country").

What do you think?

With John having read the LXX and seeing all those uses of *EKLEKTOS* there, what did he mean by saying:

> The Elder,
> To the *EKLEKTOS* lady and her children, whom I love in truth, and not only I, but also all those who have known the truth,   *2 John 1:1*

> The Elder,
> To the excellent lady and her children, whom I love in truth, and not only I, but also all those who have known the truth,
>   *2 John 1:1 JM*

Then there are doubts to examine?

Having seen the majority view of *EKLEKTOS*, let's now look at the words that at first glance might appear to put a spanner in the works; a fly in the ointment; a perceived cause for thinking this is not all there is to it.

We saw two chapters ago all the Hebrew words were at least once translated by *EKLEKTOS* in the LXX with a meaning of top quality, then, we looked at all those that consistently kept giving that meaning, a reduced number.

Four from the full list of Hebrew words have other meanings translated in the English bibles too. Those four Hebrew words I excluded from the preceding chapter so we could look at them here. So which words are these?

Four words remain, BACHAR, BACHUR, BARAR and MIBCHAR.

I will in this chapter first present them in the same manner as the others in the previous chapter, except that this time, the limited frame of reference before, of mainly the NKJV, is now without exception (below) increased to include the KJV, NASB, NIV and NLT. This then helps highlight the "doubt" as well as the "top quality" of each of those words' meaning.

I will then summarise that difference.

Then separately, in the following chapter, we will look more closely at each of these four Hebrew words and examine the seeming doubt that appears here.

So, in the first look of two chapters ago with these very four words remaining, we saw that these were used for:

BACHAR "**choice** silver", BACHUR "**young men**", BARAR "With the

pure You will show Yourself **pure**" and, MIBCHAR "the **choicest** of our burial places".

As stated, these 4 Heb. words are now presented in the same manner as the previous chapter, but with added sources of reference: not just the NKJV, but also KJV, NASB, NIV and NLT:

BACHAR
"**choice** silver" – choice, best **OR** chosen, selected, choose

As well as Proverbs 8:19 (1-8) the other places where it is translated by *EKLEKTOS* in the LXX:

Exodus 14:7   "**choice** chariots/**chosen** chariots KJV/**select** chariots NASB/**best** chariots NIV, NLT"

Judges 20:15   "**select** men/**chosen** men KJV/**choice** men NASB/ **able young** men NIV/**elite** troops NLT"

Judges 20:34   "**select** men/**chosen** men KJV/**choice** men NASB/ **able young** men NIV/**elite** . . . troops NLT"

1 Samuel 24:2   "**chosen** men/**chosen** men KJV, NASB/**able young** men NIV/**elite** troops NLT"

1 Samuel 26:2   "**chosen** men/**chosen** men KJV, NASB/**select** . . . troops NIV/**elite** troops NLT"

Psalm 89:19   "**one chosen**/*one* **chosen** KJV/**one chosen** NASB/ **a young man** NIV/**selected** NLT"

Song of Songs 5:15 "**excellent** as the cedars = KJV/**choice** . . . cedars NASB, NIV/**noble** cedars NLT"

Exodus 14:7 BACHAR (2-8)

> Also, he took six hundred **choice** chariots, and all the chariots of Egypt with captains over every one of them.

> And he took six hundred **chosen** chariots, and all the chariots of Egypt, and captains over every one of them. *KJV*

> and he took six hundred **select** chariots, and all the other chariots of Egypt with officers over all of them.   *NASB*

... **best** chariots ...   *NIV, NLT*

LXX

> *KAI LABÓN EXAKOSIA HARMATA **EKLEKTA** KAI PASAN*
> and he took six hundred   chariots   choice   and   all
>
> *TÉN HIPPON TÓN AIGUPTIÓN KAI TRISTATAS*
> the   horse of the Egyptians   and   tribunes
>
> *EPI PANTÓN*
> over   all

engLXX

> having also taken six hundred chosen chariots, and all the
> cavalry of the Egyptians, and rulers over all.

Judges 20:15 BACHAR (3-8)

> And from their cities at that time the children of Benjamin
> numbered twenty-six thousand men who drew the sword,
> besides the inhabitants of Gibeah, who numbered seven
> hundred **select** men.

> And the children of Benjamin were numbered at that
> time out of the cities twenty and six thousand men that
> drew sword, beside the inhabitants of Gibeah, which were
> numbered seven hundred **chosen** men.   *KJV*

> From the cities on that day the sons of Benjamin were
> numbered, 26,000 men who draw the sword, besides the
> inhabitants of Gibeah who were numbered, 700 **choice** men.
>   *NASB*

> At once the Benjaminites mobilised twenty-six thousand
> swordsmen from their towns, in addition to seven hundred
> **able young** men from those living in Gibeah.   *NIV*

> In all, 26,000 of their warriors armed with swords arrived
> in Gibeah to join the 700 **elite** troops who lived there. *NLT*

LXX

KAI EPESKEPÉSAN HOI HUIOI BENIAMIN EN TÉ
and   numbered   the   sons of Benjamin in the

HÉMERA EKEINÉ APO TÓN POLEÓN EIKOSITREIS
day   that   from the   cities   twenty three

CHILIADES ANÉR HELKÓN RHOMPHAIAN EKTOS TÓN
thousand man wounding   sword   without of the

OIKOUNTÓN TÉN GABAA HOI EPESKEPÉSAN HEPTAKOSIOI
dwellers of the Gabaa the   numbered   seven hundred

*ANDRES **EKLEKTOI** EK PANTOS LAOU*
men   choice   out of all   people

AMPHOTERODEXIOI
ambidextruous

engLXX

And the children of Benjamin from their cities were numbered
in that day, twenty-three thousand, every man drawing a
sword, besides the inhabitants of Gabaa, who were numbered
seven hundred chosen men of all the people, able to use both
hands alike;

Judges 20:34 BACHAR (4-8)

And ten thousand **select** men from all Israel came against
Gibeah, and the battle was fierce. But the Benjamites did not
know that disaster *was* upon them.

And there came against Gibeah ten thousand **chosen** men
out of all Israel, and the battle was sore: but they knew not
that evil *was* near them.   *KJV*

When ten thousand **choice** men from all Israel came
against Gibeah, the battle became fierce; but Benjamin did
not know that disaster was close to them.   *NASB*

Then ten thousand of Israel's able young men made a

frontal attack on Gibeah. The fighting was so heavy that the Benjaminites did not realise how near disaster was. *NIV*

There were 10,000 elite Israelite troops who advanced against Gibeah. The fighting was so heavy that Benjamin didn't realize the impending disaster. *NLT*

LXX

KAI ÉLTHON EXENANTIAS GABAA DEKA CHILIADES
and came out of opposite Gabaa ten thousand

*ANDRÓN **EKLEKTÓN** EK PANTOS ISRAÉL KAI*
of men choice out of of all Israel and

PARATAXIS BAREIA KAI AUTOI OUK EGNÓSAN HOTI
side by side heavy and they not know since

PHTHANEI AP AUTOUS HÉ KAKIA
come upon them the evil

engLXX

And there came over against Gabaa ten thousand chosen men out of all Israel; and the fight *was* severe; and they knew not that evil was coming upon them.

---

1 Samuel 24:2 BACHAR (5-8)

Then Saul took three thousand **chosen** men from all Israel, and went to seek David and his men on the Rocks of the Wild Goats.

... **chosen** men ... *KJV, NASB*

... three thousand **able young** men ... *NIV*

... 3,000 **elite** troops from all Israel ... *NLT*

LXX 1 Kings 24:3

[In the LXX 1 Samuel = 1 Kings, 2 Samuel = 2 Kings, 1 Kings = 3 Kings & 2 Kings = 4 Kings]

KAI ELABE METH HEAUTOU TREIS CHILIADAS
and took with himself three thousand

*ANDRÓN **EKLEKTOUS** EK PANTOS ISRAÉL KAI*
men   choice   out of   all   Israel and

EPOREUTHÉ ZÉTEIN TON DAUID KAI TOUS ANDRAS
  went   to seek the David and the   men

AUTOU EPI PROSÓPON SADDAIEM
of him upon   face   of Saddæem

engLXX
> And he took with him three thousand men, chosen out of all Israel, and went to seek David and his men in front of Saddæem.

---

1 Samuel 26:2 BACHAR (6-8)

> Then Saul arose and went down to the Wilderness of Ziph, having three thousand **chosen** men of Israel with him, to seek David in the Wilderness of Ziph.

. . . three thousand **chosen** men of Israel . . .	*KJV, NASB*
. . . three thousand **select** Israelite **troops** . . .	*NIV*
. . . 3,000 of Israel's **elite troops** . . .	*NLT*

LXX   1 Kings 26:2
[In the LXX 1 Samuel = 1 Kings, 2 Samuel = 2 Kings, 1 Kings = 3 Kings & 2 Kings = 4 Kings]

KAI ANESTÉ SAOUL KAI KATEBÉ EIS TÉN ERÉMON ZIPH
and arose   Saul and   went into the   desert of Ziph

KAI MET AUTOU TREIS CHILIADES ANDRÓN
and with him   three   thousand of men

***EKLEKTOI** EX ISRAÉL ZÉTEIN TON DAUID EN TÉ*
  choice   out of Israel to seek the David in the
ERÉMÓ ZIPH
 desert of Ziph

engLXX
> And Saul arose, and went down to the wilderness of Ziph, and

with him *went* three thousand men chosen out of Israel, to seek David in the wilderness of Ziph.

Psalm 89:19 BACHAR (7-8)

Then You spoke in a vision to Your holy one, and said: "I have given help to *one who* is mighty; I have exalted **one chosen** from the people.

Then thou spakest in vision to thy holy one, and saidst, I have laid help upon *one that is* mighty; I have exalted *one* **chosen** out of the people. *KJV*

Once You spoke in vision to Your godly ones, and said, "I have given help to one who is mighty; I have exalted **one chosen** from the people. *NASB*

Once you spoke in a vision, to your faithful people you said: "I have bestowed strength on a warrior; I have raised up **a young man** from among the people. *NIV*

Long ago you spoke in a vision to your faithful people. You said, "I have raised up a warrior. I have **selected** him from the common people to be king. *NLT*

LXX 88:19

TOTE ELALÉSAS EN HORASEI TOIS HUIOIS SOU KAI EIPAS
then   spoke   in   vision to the sons of you and said

ETHEMÉN BOÉTHEIAN EPI DUNATON HUPSÓSA
placed   aid   upon mighty   raising

EKLEKTON *EK TOU LAOU MOU*
choice   out of the people of me

engLXX

Then thou spokest in vision to thy children, and saidst, I have laid help on a mighty one; I have exalted one chosen out of my people.

Song of Songs 5:15 BACHAR (8-8)

His legs *are* pillars of marble set on bases of fine gold. His countenance *is* like Lebanon, **excellent** as the cedars.

... **excellent** as the cedars.	KJV
... **choice** as the cedars.	NASB
... **choice** as its cedars.	NIV
... like the **noble** cedars of Lebanon.	NLT

LXX

KNÉMAI AUTOU STULOI MARMARINOI
   legs   of him columns   marble

TETHEMELIÓMENOI EPI BASEIS CHRUSAS EIDOS
   founded   upon bases of gold   form

*AUTOU HÓS LIBANOS **EKLEKTOS** HÓS KEDROI*
  of him as Lebanon   choice   as cedars

engLXX
His legs are marble pillars set on golden sockets: his form is as Libanus, choice as the cedars.

Of the 172 instances of BACHAR in the LXX **8** are given as ***EKLEKTOS***, 113 are *EKLEGÓ* (to choose, pick), 12 are *HAIRETIZÓ* (to choose), 6 are *EPILEGÓ* (pick out, select), 4 are *DUNATOS* (strong, mighty, able), 4 are *NEANIAS* (young man, youth), 3 are *HAIREÓ* (to choose, prefer), 2 are *DIAKRINÓ* (judge, decide), 2 are *EPHISTÉMI* (set up, establish), 2 are *EXAIREÓ* (to choose, select out), 2 are *HAIRETOS* *not in the NT* (to be chosen, elected), 2 are *PROAIREÓ* (to choose, prefer), 1 is *APALLASSÓ* (set free), 1 is *ARESKÓ* (to do what pleases), 1 is *ARESTOS* (acceptable, pleasing), 1 is *DOKIMAZÓ* (to approve, assay), 1 is *EPITHUMEÓ* (desired, coveted), 1 is *METOCHOS* (partaking), 1 is *NEANISKOS* (young man, boy), 1 is *PUROÓ* (to burn with fire, purge), 1 is *ZÉLOÓ* (to esteem, emulate) and, 3 are not translated.

All the references for BACHAR are:

Genesis 6:2; Genesis 13:11; **Exodus 14:7**; Exodus 17:9; Exodus 18:25; Numbers 16:5; Numbers 16:7; Numbers 17:5; Deuteronomy 4:37; Deuteronomy 7:6; Deuteronomy 7:7; Deuteronomy 10:15; Deuteronomy 12:5; Deuteronomy 12:11; Deuteronomy 12:14; Deuteronomy 12:18; Deuteronomy 12:21; Deuteronomy 12:26; Deuteronomy 14:2; Deuteronomy 14:23; Deuteronomy 14:24; Deuteronomy 14:25; Deuteronomy 15:20; Deuteronomy 16:2; Deuteronomy 16:6; Deuteronomy 16:7; Deuteronomy 16:11; Deuteronomy 16:15; Deuteronomy 16:16; Deuteronomy 17:8; Deuteronomy 17:10; Deuteronomy 17:15; Deuteronomy 18:5; Deuteronomy 18:6; Deuteronomy 21:5; Deuteronomy 23:16; Deuteronomy 26:2; Deuteronomy 30:19; Deuteronomy 31:11; Joshua 8:3; Joshua 9:27; Joshua 24:15; Joshua 24:22; Judges 5:8; Judges 10:14; **Judges 20:15**; Judges 20:16; **Judges 20:34**; 1 Samuel 2:28; 1 Samuel 8:18; 1 Samuel 10:24; 1 Samuel 12:13; 1 Samuel 13:2; 1 Samuel 16:8; 1 Samuel 16:9; 1 Samuel 16:10; 1 Samuel 17:40; 1 Samuel 20:30; **1Samuel 24:2**; **1Samuel 26:2**; 2 Samuel 6:1; 2 Samuel 6:21; 2 Samuel 10:9a; 2 Samuel 10:9b; 2 Samuel 15:15; 2 Samuel 16:18; 2 Samuel 17:1; 2 Samuel 19:38; 2 Samuel 24:12; 1 Kings 3:8; 1 Kings 8:16a; 1 Kings 8:16b; 1 Kings 8:44; 1 Kings 8:48; 1 Kings 11:13; 1 Kings 11:32; 1 Kings 11:34; 1 Kings 11:36; 1 Kings 12:21; 1 Kings 14:21; 1 Kings 18:23; 1 Kings 18:25; 2 Kings 21:7; 2 Kings 23:27; 1 Chronicles 15:2; 1 Chronicles 19:10a; 1 Chronicles 19:10b; 1 Chronicles 21:10; 1 Chronicles 28:4a; 1 Chronicles 28:4b; 1 Chronicles 28:5; 1 Chronicles 28:6; 1 Chronicles 28:10; 1 Chronicles 29:1; 2 Chronicles 6:5a; 2 Chronicles 6:5b; 2 Chronicles 6:6a; 2 Chronicles 6:6b; 2 Chronicles 6:34; 2 Chronicles 6:38; 2 Chronicles 7:12; 2 Chronicles 7:16; 2 Chronicles 11:1; 2 Chronicles 12:13; 2 Chronicles 13:3a; 2 Chronicles 13:3b; 2 Chronicles 13:17; 2 Chronicles 25:5; 2 Chronicles 29:11; 2 Chronicles 33:7; Nehemiah 1:9; Nehemiah 9:7; Job 7:15; Job 9:14; Job 15:5; Job 29:25; Job 34:4; Job 34:33; Job 36:21; Psalm 25:12; Psalm 33:12; Psalm 47:4; Psalm 65:4; Psalm 78:67; Psalm 78:68; Psalm 78:70; Psalm 84:10; **Psalm 89:19**; Psalm 105:26; Psalm 119:30; Psalm 119:173; Psalm 132:13; Psalm 135:4; Proverbs 1:29; Proverbs 3:31; Proverbs 8:10; **Proverbs 8:19**; Proverbs 10:20; Proverbs 16:16; Proverbs 21:3; Proverbs 22:1; Ecclesiastes 9:4; **Song of Songs 5:15**; Isaiah 1:29; Isaiah 7:15; Isaiah 7:16; Isaiah 14:1;

Isaiah 40:20; Isaiah 41:8; Isaiah 41:9; Isaiah 41:24; Isaiah 43:10; Isaiah 44:1; Isaiah 44:2; Isaiah 48:10; Isaiah 49:7; Isaiah 56:4; Isaiah 58:5; Isaiah 58:6; Isaiah 65:12; Isaiah 66:3; Isaiah 66:4a; Isaiah 66:4b; Jeremiah 8:3; Jeremiah 33:24; Jeremiah 49:19; Jeremiah 50:44; Ezekiel 20:5; Haggai 2:23; Zechariah 1:17; Zechariah 2:12; Zechariah 3:2

BACHUR

"**young men**" – guys in their prime and fit to be soldiers

As well as 2 Kings 8:12 (1-5) the other places where it is translated by *EKLEKTOS* in the LXX:

Psalm 78:31	"**choice** *men*/**chosen** KJV"
Lamentations 1:15	"**young men/young warriors** NLT"
Lamentations 5:13	"**young men**"
Lamentations 5:14	"**young men**"

Psalm 78:31 BACHUR (2-5)

> The wrath of God came against them, and slew the stoutest of them, and struck down the **choice** *men* of Israel.

> The wrath of God came upon them, and slew the fattest of them, and smote down **the chosen** *men* of Israel.　　　　*KJV*

> The anger of God rose against them and killed some of their stoutest ones, and subdued the **choice men** of Israel.
> 　　　　　　　　　　　　　　　　　　　　　　*NASB*

> God's anger rose against them; he put to death the sturdiest among them, cutting down the **young men** of Israel. *NIV*

> the anger of God rose against them, and he killed their strongest men. He struck down the **finest** of Israel's **young men**.　　　　　　　　　　　　　　　　　　　　*NLT*

LXX 77:31
> *KAI ORGÉ TOU THEOU ANEBÉ EP AUTOUS KAI*
> and anger of the God 　 arose upon them 　 and

APEKTEINEN EN TOIS PIOSIN AUTÓN KAI TOUS
   killed   in   the plenty of them and the

EKLEKTOUS *TOU ISRAÉL SUNEPODISEN*
  choice   of the Israel   bound feet

engLXX

then the indignation of God rose up against them, and slew the fattest of them, and overthrew the choice men of Israel.

Lamentations 1:15 BACHUR (3-5)

"The Lord has trampled underfoot all my mighty *men* in my midst; He has called an assembly against me to crush my **young men**; the Lord trampled *as* in a winepress the virgin daughter of Judah. 16For these *things* I weep; (. . .)

  . . . young men . . .   *KJV, NASB, NIV*

"The Lord has treated my mighty men with contempt. At his command a great army has come to crush my **young warriors**. The Lord has trampled his beloved city like grapes are trampled in a winepress. 16For all these things I weep; (. . .)   *NLT*

LXX

SAMECH

EXÉRE PANTAS TOUS ISCHHROUS MOU HO KURIOS EK
 lift out   all   the   strong   of me the Lord out of

MESOU MOU EKALESEN EP EME KAIRON TOU
 midst of me called upon me season of the

SUNTRIPSAI **EKLEKTOUS** *MOU LÉNON EPATÉSE*
 to break   choice   of me vat   trod

KURIOS PARTHENÓ THUGATRI IOUDA EPI TOUTOIS
 Lord   for virgin daughter of Juda upon for these

EGÓ KLAIÓ
 I   weep

engLXX

SAMECH

The Lord has cut off all my strong men from the midst of me: he has summoned against me a time for crushing my choice men: the Lord has trodden a wine-press for the virgin daughter of Juda: for these things I weep.

Lamentations 5:13 BACHUR (4-5)

Young men ground at the millstones; boys staggered under *loads of* wood.

. . . **young men** . . .   *KJV, NASB, NIV, NLT*

LXX

EKLEKTOI KLAUTHMON ANELABON KAI NEANISKOI
   choice   weeping   raised and young men
EN XULÓ ÉSTHENÉSAN
  in tree   weakened

engLXX

The chosen men lifted up *the voice in* weeping, and the youths fainted under the wood.

Lamentations 5:14 BACHUR (5-5)

The elders have ceased *gathering at* the gate, and the **young men** from their music.

. . . **young men** . . .   *KJV, NASB, NIV, NLT*

LXX

*KAI PRESBUTAI APO PULÉS KATEPAUSAN **EKLEKTOI***
 and   elders   from gate   ceased   choice
EK PSALMÓN AUTÓN KATEPAUSAN
 out of psalms of them   ceased

engLXX

And the elders ceased from the gate, the chosen men ceased

from their music.

Of the 45 instances of BACHUR in the LXX **5** are given as ***EKLEKTOS***, 34 are *NEANISKOS* (young man, boy), 2 are *NEANIAS* (young man, youth), 1 is *ANÉR* (particular man, husband) and, 3 are not translated.

All the references for BACHUR are:
Deuteronomy 32:25; Judges 14:10; Ruth 3:10; 1 Samuel 8:16; 1 Samuel 9:2; **2 Kings 8:12**; 2 Chronicles 36:17a; 2 Chronicles 36:17b; **Psalm 78:31**; Psalm 78:63; Psalm 148:12; Proverbs 20:29; Ecclesiastes 11:9; Isaiah 9:17; Isaiah 23:4; Isaiah 31:8; Isaiah 40:30; Isaiah 42:22; Isaiah 62:5; Jeremiah 6:11; Jeremiah 9:21; Jeremiah 11:22; Jeremiah 15:8; Jeremiah 18:21; Jeremiah 31:13; Jeremiah 48:15; Jeremiah 49:26; Jeremiah 50:30; Jeremiah 51:3; Jeremiah 51:22; **Lamentations 1:15**; Lamentations 1:18; Lamentations 2:21; **Lamentations 5:13; Lamentations 5:14**; Ezekiel 9:6; Ezekiel 23:6; Ezekiel 23:12; Ezekiel 23:23; Ezekiel 30:17; Joel 2:28; Amos 2:11; Amos 4:10; Amos 8:13; Zechariah 9:17

BARAR
"**pure . . . pure**" – pure, choice, clean

As well as 2 Samuel 22:27(a & b - 1&2-8) the other places where it is translated by *EKLEKTOS* in the LXX:
1 Chronicles 7:40 "**choice men**, mighty men of valor/**select men** NLT"
1 Chronicles 9:22 "**chosen** as gatekeepers/**listed** NLT"
Nehemiah 5:18 "**choice** sheep"
Psalm18:26 "With the **pure** You will show Yourself **pure**"
Isaiah 49:2 "a **polished** shaft/**select** arrow NASB/**polished** arrow NIV/**sharp** arrow NLT"

1 Chronicles 7:40 BARAR (3-8)

> All these *were* the children of Asher, heads of *their* fathers' houses, **choice men**, mighty men of valor, chief leaders. And they were recorded by genealogies among the army fit

for battle; their number *was* twenty-six thousand.

. . . **choice** *and* mighty men of valour, chief of the princes. . .
KJV

. . . **choice** and mighty men of valor, heads of the princes. . .
NASB

. . . heads of families, **choice men**, brave warriors and outstanding leaders. . .
NIV

. . . They were all **select men**—mighty warriors and outstanding leaders. . .
NLT

LXX

PANTES HOUTOI HUIOI ASÉR PANTES ARCHONTES
   all   these   sons of Aser all   chiefs

*PATRIÓN **EKLEKTOI** ISCHUROI DUNAMEI ARCHONTES*
of families   choice   strong   powerful   chiefs

HÉGOUMENOI HO ARITHMOS AUTÓN EIS PARATAXIN
  leading   the   number of them into   array
TOU POLEMEIN ARITHMOS AUTÓN ANDRES EIKOSIEX
of the   war   number   of them   men   twenty-six

CHILIADES
 thousand

engLXX

All these were the sons of Aser, all heads of families, choice, mighty men, chief leaders: their number for battle array- their number was twenty-six thousand men.

---

1 Chronicles 9:22 BARAR (4-8)

All those **chosen** as gatekeepers *were* two hundred and twelve. They were recorded by their genealogy, in their villages. David and Samuel the seer had appointed them to their trusted office.

. . . **chosen** . . .
KJV, NASB, NIV

In all, there were 212 gatekeepers in those days, and they were **listed** according to the genealogies in their villages. David and Samuel the seer had appointed their ancestors because they were reliable men. *NLT*

LXX

*PANTES HOI **EKLEKTOI** EPI TÉS PULÉS EN TAIS PULAIS*
all   the   choice upon the gate in the gates

DIAKOSIOI KAI DEKADUO HOUTOI EN TAIS AULAIS
two-hundred and twelve   these in the courts

AUTÓN HO KATALOCHISMOS AUTÓN TOUTOUS ESTÉSE
of them the   distribution   of them   these established

DAUID KAI SAMOUÉL HO BLEPÓN TÉ PISTEI AUTÓN
David and   Samuel the seer   the trust of *them*

engLXX

All the chosen porters in the gates *were* two hundred and twelve, these *were* in their courts, *this* was their distribution: these David and Samuel the seer established in their charge.

Nehemiah 5:18 BARAR (5-8)

Now *that* which was prepared *for me* daily *was* one ox *and* six **choice** sheep; also fowl were prepared for me, and once every ten days an abundance of all kinds of wine; yet in spite of this I did not demand the governor's provisions, because the bondage was heavy on this people.

… **choice** sheep …   *KJV, NASB, NIV, NLT*

LXX

KAI ÉN GINOMENON EIS HÉMERAN MIAN MOSCHOS
and was   coming into   day   one   calf

*EIS KAI PROBATA EX **EKLEKTA** KAI CHIMAROS*
into and sheep out of choice   and male goat

EGINONTO MOI KAI ANAMESON DEKA HÉMERÓN EN
came   to me and   in midst   ten   days   in

PASIN OINOS TÓ PLÉTHEI KAI SUN TOUTOIS ARTOUS
all   wine for the multitude and with   these   bread

TÉS BIAS OUK EZÉTÉSA HOTI BAREIA HÉ DOULEIA
of the force not   seek   since heavy the slavery

EPI TON LAON TOUTON
upon the people   this

engLXX

And there came to *me* for one day one calf, and I had six choice sheep and a goat; and every ten days wine in abundance of all sorts: yet with these I required not the bread of extortion, because the bondage was heavy upon this people.

Psalm 18:26 BARAR (6-8; 7-8)

With the **pure** You will show Yourself **pure**; and with the devious You will show Yourself shrewd.

... **pure** ... **pure** ...   *KJV, NASB, NIV, NLT*

LXX 17:26

*KAI META **EKLEKTOU EKLEKTOS** ESÉ KAI META*
and with   choice   choice shall be and with

STREBLOU DIASTREPSEIS
crooked shall turn aside from

engLXX

And with the excellent *man* thou wilt be excellent; and with the perverse thou wilt shew frowardness.

Isaiah 49:2 BARAR (8-8)

And He has made My mouth like a sharp sword; in the shadow of His hand He has hidden Me, and made Me a **polished** shaft; in His quiver He has hidden Me."

... a **polished** shaft ...   *KJV*

... a **select** arrow ...   NASB

... a **polished** arrow ...   NIV

... a **sharp** arrow in his quiver ...   NLT

LXX

KAI ETHÉKE TO STOMA MOU HÓS MACHAIRAN
and   made   the   mouth of me as   sword

OXEIAN KAI HUPO TÉN SKEPÉN TÉS CHEIROS AUTOU
sharp   and under the protection of the hand   of him

*EKRUPSE ME ETHÉKE ME HÓS BELOS **EKLEKTON** KAI*
hid   me   made me as arrow   choice   and

EN TÉ PHARETRA AUTOU EKRUPSE ME
in the   quiver   of him   hid   me

engLXX

and he has made my mouth as a sharp sword, and he has hid me under

the shadow of his hand; he has made me as a choice shaft, and he has
hid me in his quiver;

Of the 18 instances of BARAR in the LXX **8** are given as **EKLEKTOS**,
2 are *EKLEGÓ* (to pick, choose), 2 are *KATHAROS* (clean, pure), 2 are
PUROÓ (burn up, purify), 1 is *APHORIZÓ* (to define, determine), 1 is
DIAKRINÓ (to decide, judge), 1 is *PARASKEUAZÓ* (make ready) and,
1 is not translated.

All the references for BARAR are:
2 Samuel 22:27a; 2 Samuel 22:27b; 1 Chronicles 7:40; 1 Chronicles 9:22;
1 Chronicles 16:41; **Nehemiah 5:18;** Job 33:3; **Psalm 18:26a;**
Psalm 18:26b; Ecclesiastes 3:18; **Isaiah 49:2;** Isaiah 52:11;
Jeremiah 4:11; Jeremiah 51:11; Ezekiel 20:38; Daniel 11:35; Daniel 12:10;
Zephaniah 3:9

MIBCHAR

"the **choicest** of our burial places" – choice, choicest

As well as Genesis 23:6 (1-7) the other places where it is translated by *EKLEKTOS* in the LXX:

Deuteronomy 12:11 "**choice** (offerings)"

Isaiah 22:7   "**choicest** valleys/**beautiful** valleys NLT"

Jeremiah 22:7   "**choice** cedars/**choicest** cedars NASB/**fine** cedar beams NIV, NLT"

Jeremiah 48:15   "**chosen/choicest** young men NASB /**finest** young men NIV/**most promising** youth NLT"

Ezekiel 31:16   "the **choice** and best/the **choicest** and best NASB, NIV/the **most beautiful** NLT"

Daniel 11:15   "**choice** troops/**chosen** KJV/their **choicest** troops NASB/the **best** troops NIV, NLT"

Deuteronomy 12:11 MIBCHAR (2-7)

> then there will be the place where the LORD your God chooses to make His name abide. There you shall bring all that I command you: your burnt offerings, your sacrifices, your tithes, the heave offerings of your hand, and all your **choice** offerings which you vow to the LORD.

... **choice** ...   *KJV, NASB, NIV*

(The NLT does not translate MIBCHAR in this passage)

LXX

KAI ESTAI HO TOPOS HON AN EKLEXÉTAI KURIOS HO
and shall be the   place which ever   chooses   Lord   the

THEOS SOU EPIKLÉTHÉNAI TO ONOMA AUTOU EKEI
 God of you   called   the   name   of him there

EKEI OISETE PANTA HOSA EGÓ ENTELLOMAI HUMIN
there bring ye   all   as many as I   charge   to you

SÉMERON TA HOLOKAUTÓMATA HUMÓN KAI TA
   today   the whole burnt offerings of you   and the

THUSIASMATA HUMÓN KAI TA EPIDEKATA HUMÓN
   sacrifices   of you and the   tithes   of you

KAI TAS APARCHAS TÓN CHEIRÓN HUMÓN KAI PAN
and the first fruits of the hands   of you and all

EKLEKTON *TÓN DÓRÓN HUMÓN HOSA AN*
   choice   of the   gifts   of you as many as ever

EUXÉSTHE KURIÓ TÓ THEÓ HUMÓN
  ye vow   to Lord the God   of you

engLXX

> And there shall be a place which the Lord thy God shall choose for his name to be called there, thither shall ye bring all things that I order you to-day; your whole-burnt-offerings, and your sacrifices, and your tithes, and the first-fruits of your hands, and every choice gift of yours, whatsoever ye shall vow to the Lord your God.

Isaiah 22:7 MIBCHAR (3-7)

It shall come to pass *that* **your choicest valleys shall be full of chariots, and the horsemen shall set themselves in array at the gate.**

. . . choicest valleys. . .   *KJV, NASB, NIV*

Chariots fill your beautiful valleys, and charioteers storm your gates.   *NLT*

LXX

*KAI ESONTAI HAI **EKLEKTAI** PHARAGGES SOU*
  and will be   the   choice   ravines of you

PLÉSTHÉSONTAI HARMATÓN HOI DE HIPPEIS
    filled   of chariots   the but horsemen

EMPHRAXOUSI TAS PULAS SOU
    block   the gates of you

engLXX
> And it shall be that thy choice valleys shall be filled with chariots, and horsemen shall block up thy gates.

Jeremiah 22:7 MIBCHAR (4-7)

I will prepare destroyers against you, everyone with his weapons; they shall cut down your **choice** cedars and cast *them* into the fire.

... **choice** cedars ...	*KJV*
... **choicest** cedars ...	*NASB*
... **fine** cedar beams ...	*NIV, NLT*

LXX
> *KAI EPAXÓ EPI SE OLOTHREUONTA ANDRA KAI TON*
> and bring upon you annihilating   man   and the
>
> *PELEKUN AUTOU KAI EKKOPSOUSI TAS **EKLEKTAS***
> axe   of him and   cut down   the choice
> *KEDROUS KAI SOU EMBALOUSIN EIS TO PUR*
> cedars and of you put   into the fire

engLXX
> and I will bring upon thee a destroying man, and his axe: and they shall cut down thy choice cedars, and cast *them* into the fire.

Jeremiah 48:15 MIBCHAR (5-7)

Moab is plundered and gone up *from* her cities; her **chosen** young men have gone down to the slaughter," says the King, whose name *is* the LORD of hosts.

... **chosen** young men ...	*KJV*

... **choicest** young men ...   *NASB*

... **finest** young men ...   *NIV*

... **most promising** youth ...   *NLT*

LXX 31:15 [See DEiTB for the list of differences between the placements of passages in Jeremiah]

*ÓLETO MÓAB POLIS AUTOU KAI **EKLEKTOI***
destroyed Moab cities   of it   and   choice

NEANISKOI AUTOU KATEBÉSAN EIS SPHAGÉN
young men of him   went down to slaughter

engLXX

Moab is ruined, *even* his city, and his choice young men have gone down to slaughter.

Ezekiel 31:16 MIBCHAR (6-7)

I made the nations shake at the sound of its fall, when I cast it down to hell together with those who descend into the Pit; and all the trees of Eden, the **choice** and best of Lebanon, all that drink water, were comforted in the depths of the earth.

... the **choice** and best of Lebanon ...   *KJV*

... the **choicest** and best of Lebanon ...   *NASB, NIV*

... the **most beautiful** and the best of Lebanon ...   *NLT*

LXX

APO TÉS PHÓNÉS TÉS PTÓSEÓS AUTOU ESEISTHÉSAN
from the sound of the fall   of him   shook

TA ETHNÉ HOTE KATEBIBAZON AUTON EIS HADOU
the nations when brought down   him   into Hades

META TÓN KATABAINONTÓN EIS LAKKON KAI
 with the   going down   into pit   and

PAREKALOUN AUTON EN GÉ[1] PANTA TA XULA TÉS
   comfort   him   in earth all   the trees of the

*TRUPHÉS KAI TA **EKLEKTA** TOU LIBANOU PANTA TA*
   luxuries and the   choice   of the Lebanon   all   the

PINONTA HUDÓR
   drinking   water

engLXX

At the sound of his fall the nations quaked, when I brought him down to Hades with them that go down to the pit: and all the trees of Delight comforted him in the heart[1], and the choice plants of Libanus, all that drink water.

[1]Likely a literal typo error in the engLXX since GÉ means "land/earth", so that the "h" in front of "heart" should be at the end: and thus read "earth".

Daniel 11:15 MIBCHAR (7-7)

"So the king of the North shall come and build a siege mound, and take a fortified city; and the forces of the South shall not withstand *him*. Even his **choice** troops *shall have no strength to resist.*

. . . his **chosen** people . . .	*KJV*
. . . their **choicest** troops . . .	*NASB*
. . . **best** troops . . .	*NIV, NLT*

LXX

KAI EISELEUSETAI BASILEUS TOU BORRA KAI EKCHEEI
  and   enter   king   of the north and pour out

PROSCHÓMA KAI SULLÉPSETAI POLEIS OCHURAS KAI
   mounds   and   seize   cities   strong and

HOI BRACHIONES TOU BASILEÓS TOU NOTOU
  the   arms   of the   king of the south

*STÉSONTAI KAI ANASTÉSONTAI HOI **EKLEKTOI***
  stand   and   arise   the   choice

AUTOU KAI OUK ESTAI ISCHUS TOU STÉNAI
of him   and not shall be strength of the to stand

engLXX

And the king of the north shall come in, and cast up a mound, and take strong cities: and the arms of the king of the south shall withstand, and his chosen ones shall rise up, but there shall be no strength to stand.

Of the 12 instances of MIBCHAR in the LXX 7 are **EKLEKTOS**, 3 are *EPILEKTOS* *not in the NT* (choice), 1 is *KALLOS* *not in the NT* (beauty) and, 1 is not translated.

All the references for MIBCHAR are:
Genesis 23:6; Exodus 15:4; **Deuteronomy 12:11**; **Isaiah 22:7**; Isaiah 37:24; **Jeremiah 22:7**; **Jeremiah 48:15**; Ezekiel 23:7; Ezekiel 24:4; Ezekiel 24:5; **Ezekiel 31:16**; **Daniel 11:15**

CLEAR
What is clear on the range of "top quality" meaning:

These four words BACHAR, BACHUR, BARAR and MIBCHAR give us more words in English to add to the previous summaries in regards to top quality.

We saw that the 1st list, two chapters ago gave us:

MIBCHAR (**choicest**), BARI (**fat**), DEROR (**liquid/pure** myrrh KJV), BECHURIM/BECHUROTH (**choice men/young men** KJV), BARAR (**pure + pure**), BACHUR (**young men**), MIBCHOR (**choice**), GELAL (**heavy** stones), MANAMMIM (**delicacies**), BACHAR (**choice** silver), CHARUTS (**diligent**), BAR (**favourite/ choice** KJV/**pure** *child* NASB), NESHEQ (**armor** of the House), BO-CHAN (**tried** stone), CHEPHETS (**precious** stones), CHEMDAH/ CHAMUDOTH (**pleasant** land), MATSOR (**fortress/bulwark** YLT), TSEBI (**beauty**), TSAMMERETH (**highest branches**), PERI (**fruit**), CHOPHESH (**saddlecloths/precious** clothes KJV), BEROMIM (**multicolored apparel**), MASETH (**taxes/ burdens** of wheat KJV).

Then, added to those was the list from the preceding chapter:
BAR ("**clear/pure** NASB/**bright** as the sun NIV"), BARI ("**fatted** oxen", "food **plentious**", "**plump**" two times &, "**fat**" a further 4 times), CHEMDAH/CHAMUDOTH ("**precious** vessel", "**Desire** of All Nations", "**pleasant** land"), PERI ("**fruit**" 1 more time), TSEBI ("**glory** of the country").

To these we could add (only) the top quality elements from the present chapter, as follows:

BACHAR

BACHAR: "**choice** chariots", "**select** chariots - NASB", "**best** chariots - NIV, NLT", "**choice** men - NASB" 2 times, "**select** men" 2 times, "**able young** men - NIV" 3 times, "**elite troops** - NLT" 4 times, "**select** . . . **troops** - NIV", "**a young man** - NIV", "**excellent** as the cedars", "**choice** . . . cedars - NASB, NIV", "**noble** cedars - NLT"

But, BACHAR was also seen above as:
"**chosen** men" X two, "**chosen** chariots - KJV", "**chosen** men – KJV" X four, "chosen men - NASB" X two, **one chosen/**one **chosen** KJV/**one chosen** NASB, **selected** NLT"

BACHUR

BACHUR: "**choice** *men*" + "**young men**" 3 more times/**young warriors** NLT

But, BACHUR was also seen above as:
"**chosen** KJV"

BARAR

BARAR: ("**pure**" 2 more times, "**choice men**, mighty men of valor", "**choice** sheep", "a **polished** shaft", "**select men** NLT" and, "a **polished** shaft/**select** arrow NASB/**polished** arrow NIV/**sharp** arrow NLT")

But, BARAR was also seen above as:
"**chosen** as gatekeepers/**listed** NLT"

MIBCHAR

MIBCHAR "**choice** (offerings)", "**choicest** valleys/**beautiful** valleys

NLT" X2, "**choicest** young men NASB/**finest** young men NIV/**most promising** youth NLT", "the **choice** and best/the **choicest** and best NASB, NIV/the **most beautiful** NLT" and, "**choice** troops/their **choicest** troops NASB/the **best** troops NIV, NLT"

But, MIBCHAR was also seen above as:
"**chosen**" and, "**chosen** KJV"

But, the addition of these top quality meanings of these four Hebrew words is fully dependent on (i.e. if) those are valid: that is, over and above the doubt brought in by the occasions where "**chosen**" was seen.

So, let's examine those doubts.

Doubts examined more closely

DOUBT?

From the four words highlighted in the preceding chapter we saw a mixture of a top quality meaning and some occasions in some bible versions where "**chosen**" was given in the English translation of the Hebrew word.

The four words were BACHAR, BACHUR, BARAR and, MIBCHAR.

Are these "**chosen**" examples proof of a valid other meaning for *EKLEKTOS*?

Let's look at them in order.

BACHAR

The meaning for BACHAR under the heading in the preceding chapter was given as:

> "**choice** silver" – choice, best **OR** chosen, selected, choose

The Hebrew word BACHAR is in fact the most used word in the OT for "choose" X77 and "chosen" X77 (also – both are KJV frequency). The LXX translates these with the most used various Greek verbs in the NT for saying (to) "choose" in English and the derivative "chosen". The detailed list under BACHAR in the preceding chapter shows these Greek words:

Of the 172 instances of BACHAR in the LXX:
       113 are *EKLEGÓ* (to choose, pick)
       12 are *HAIRETIZÓ* (to choose)
       6 are *EPILEGÓ* (pick out, select)
These add up to 131 "choose" and "chosen" out of 172, which is 76% of the use of BACHAR: A clear use for "chosen" and "choose"

Added to these, with little hesitation to them being of the *same* emphasis:

> 3 are *HAIREÓ* (to choose, prefer)
> 2 are *DIAKRINÓ* (judge, decide
> 2 are *PROAIREÓ* (to choose, prefer)
> 1 is *ARESKÓ* (to do what pleases)
> 1 is *APALLASSÓ* (set free)
> 1 is *ZÉLOÓ* (to esteem, emulate)
> 1 is *EPITHUMEÓ* (desired, coveted).

It can then be seen that BACHAR is well used in a whole category involving the English verb "to choose" in all its forms, including "chosen" and "selected".

This leaves us with a minor but significant set of other Greek words for which BACHAR is seen by the LXX translators to mean something different: in a category other than with the verb "to choose".

These are:

> 4 are *DUNATOS* (strong, mighty, able)

Found in:

> 2 Chronicles 13:3a; 2 Chronicles 13:3b; 2 Chronicles 13:17; 2 Chronicles 25:5

> 4 are *NEANIAS* (young man, youth)

Found in:

> 2 Samuel 6:1; 2 Samuel 10:9; 1 Kings 12:21; 1 Chronicles 19:10

> 1 is *NEANISKOS* (young man, boy)

Found in:

> 2 Chronicles 11:1

These 9 Greek word examples are distinct in not involving a choice, but a clear view of "top quality".

Added to these:

> 2 are *EPHISTÉMI* (set up, establish)
> 1 is *PUROÓ* (to burn with fire, purge)
> 1 is *DOKIMAZÓ* (to approve, assay).

In the exhaustive DEiTB I give a fuller account of all these including the following words which I leave the reader to place in either category:

> 2 are *EXAIREÓ* (to choose, select out)
> 2 are *HAIRETOS* (to be chosen, elected)
> 1 is *ARESTOS* (acceptable, pleasing)
> 1 is *METOCHOS* (partaking).

So then two meanings are in view for BACHAR

Two categories of meaning are seen by two sets of Greek verbs and words fitting into two distinct types. This is reinforced in display when they are seen used in the same passage.

That is to say the LXX translators clearly saw two separate meanings for BACHAR with both "To choose/chosen" and "the best, top quality, excellent" as seen from BACHAR.

This is no different to English with words with two meanings like "table" or "chair". Both those words have two meanings each, and though they look the same and pronounce the same each time, it is dependent on the surrounding words which of the two meanings is meant.

> "The man sat on a chair whist sitting at a table"

One meaning each for "chair" and "table". but,

> "On that table was a note to the Chair of the committee letting
> him know that the table of contents had all he needed to know."

A "chair" you sit on is not a "Chair" of a committee, neither is a "table" where you sit the same as a "table" of contents:

Two meanings from the exact same word and the immediate context of words are the only qualifier.

Here is BACHAR twice, in the same passage, with the surrounding words showing us a different meaning for the word, but also the LXX translator making use of a different Greek word to show the different meaning:

2 Samuel 10:9 – BACHAR X2

When Joab saw that the battle line was against him before and behind, he **chose** some of the **choice** *men* of Israel and put *them* in battle array against the Syrians.

LXX   2 Kings 10:9

[In the LXX 1 Samuel = 1 Kings, 2 Samuel = 2 Kings, 1 Kings = 3 Kings & 2 Kings = 4 Kings]

KAI EIDEN IÓAB HOTI EGENÉTHÉ PROS AUTON
and   saw   Joab since   it be   to   him

ANTIPROSÓPON TOU POLEMOU EK TOU KATA
     facing   the   war   out of the against

PROSÓPON EXENANTIAS KAI EK TOU OPISTHEN KAI
    face   right opposite and out of the   rear   and

EPELEXATO *EK PANTÓN TÓN* **NEANIÓN** *ISRAÉL KAI*
  chose   out of   all   the young men of Israel and

PARETAXANTO EX ENANTIAS SURIAS
  deployed   out of opposite   Syria

engLXX

And Joab saw that the front of the battle was against him from that which was opposed in front and from behind, and he chose out some of all the young men of Israel, and they set themselves in array against Syria.

      The NIV and NLT show this well in English:

NIV - 2 Samuel 10:9 – BACHAR X2

Joab saw that there were battle lines in front of him and behind him; so he **selected** some of the **best troops** in Israel and deployed them against the Arameans.

NLT - 2 Samuel 10:9 – BACHAR X2

When Joab saw that he would have to fight on both the front and the rear, he **chose** some of Israel's **elite troops** and placed them under his personal command to fight the Arameans in the fields.

As can be seen two words in a different category of meaning are used in English and in the Greek for the two occasions of BACHAR in the text. In the LXX:

EPILEGÓ (pick out, select) and *NEANIAS* (young man, youth)

The parallel passage in Chronicles also uses BACHAR twice within the same passage to the same effect:

1 Chronicles 19:10 – BACHAR X2

When Joab saw that the battle line was set against him before and behind, he chose some of the choice men of Israel and put *them* in battle array against the Syrians.

LXX

KAI EIDEN IÓAB HOTI GEGONASIN ANTIPROSÓPOI
and   saw   Joab   since   it be   face off

TOU POLEMEIN PROS AUTON KATA PROSÓPON KAI
the   war   to   him according to front   and

*EXOPISTHE KAI **EXELEXATO** EK PANTOS **NEANIOU***
behind   and   chose   out of   all   young men

EX ISRAÉL KAI PARETAXANTO ENANTION TOU SUROU
out of Israel and   set   before   the Syrian

engLXX

And Joab saw that they were fronting him to fight against him before and behind, and he chose some out of all the young men of Israel, and they set themselves in array against the Syrian.

Again the NIV and NLT show this well in English:

NIV - 1 Chronicles 19:10 – BACHAR X2

Joab saw that there were battle lines in front of him and behind him; so he selected some of the best troops in Israel and deployed them against the Arameans.

NLT - 1 Chronicles 19:10 – BACHAR X2

> When Joab saw that he would have to fight on both the front and the rear, he **chose** some of Israel's **elite troops** and placed them under his personal command to fight the Arameans in the fields.

In the LXX:

EKLEGÓ (to choose, pick) and *NEANIAS* (young man, youth)

So BACHAR has two meanings. Just like "chair" in English is more used for the piece of furniture we sit on, so BACHAR is most used for the verb "to choose" and the derivative "chosen". But the second use, though less frequent, is still very clear: something of top quality, preferred, "to be chosen, excellent". So "young men", guys in their prime as fighting soldiers in hand to hand combat, are used to translate BACHAR. Now BACHUR is the normal word for "young man" in the Hebrew and we saw in the two preceding chapters how *EKLEKTOS* is also used to translate BACHUR directly (see also below for a full list of BACHUR translated by *EKLEKTOS*).

We can see then that *EKLEKTOS* is in the same second category of words to translate BACHAR as *NEANIAS* (young man, youth), *DUNATOS* (strong, mighty, able) and *NEANISKOS* (young man, boy). *EKLEKTOS* is only for the category of "to be chosen, excellent"

BACHUR

The meaning for BACHUR under the heading in the preceding chapter is seen as:

"**young men**" – guys in their prime and fit to be soldiers

This Hebrew word BACHUR is in fact the main word for "young man" in Hebrew. The reason BACHUR is in this list is only because of the KJV where on one (1) occasion it is rendered as "chosen" in Psalm *78:31*. Here it is with 5 other English versions alongside the KJV:

Psalm 78:31 BACHUR – LXX *EKLEKTOS*

The wrath of God came against them, and slew the stoutest of them, and struck down the **choice** *men* of Israel.

The wrath of God came upon them, and slew the fattest of them, and smote down **the chosen** *men* of Israel.   *KJV*

And the anger of God hath gone up against them, and He slayeth among their fat ones, and **youths** of Israel He caused to bend.   *YLT*

The anger of God rose against them and killed some of their stoutest ones, and subdued the **choice men** of Israel. *NASB*

God's anger rose against them; he put to death the sturdiest among them, cutting down the **young men** of Israel. *NIV*

the anger of God rose against them, and he killed their strongest men. He struck down the **finest** of Israel's **young men**.   *NLT*

LXX 77:31

KAI ORGÉ TOU THEOU ANEBÉ EP AUTOUS KAI
and anger of the God   arose upon them   and

APEKTEINEN EN TOIS PIOSIN AUTÓN KAI TOUS
killed   in the   plenty of them and   the

EKLEKTOUS *TOU ISRAÉL SUNEPODISEN*
choice   of the Israel   bound feet

engLXX
then the indignation of God rose up against them, and slew the fattest of them, and overthrew the choice men of Israel.

We see then the KJV is the only version rendering BACHUR as "chosen" but, in the KJV is this rendering for BACHUR as "chosen" repeated at all?

Here are all the renderings of BACHUR
with the KJV alongside and the rendering in the LXX:

Ref.	KJV	LXX
Deuteronomy 32:25	"young man"	*NEANISKOS*
Judges 14:10	"young men"	*NEANISKOS*
Ruth 3:10	"young men"	*NEANIAS*
1 Samuel 8:16	"young men"	Not translated
1 Samuel 9:2	"young man"	*ANÉR*
2 Kings 8:12	**"young men"**	***EKLEKTOS***
2 Chronicles 36:17a	"young men"	*NEANISKOS*
2 Chronicles 36:17b	"young man"	Not translated
Psalm 78:31	**"the chosen"**	***EKLEKTOS***
Psalm 78:63	"young men"	*NEANISKOS*
Psalm 148:12	"young men"	*NEANISKOS*
Proverbs 20:29	"young men"	*NEANIAS*
Ecclesiastes 11:9	"young man"	*NEANISKOS*
Isaiah 9:17	"young men"	*NEANISKOS*
Isaiah 23:4	"young men"	*NEANISKOS*
Isaiah 31:8	"young men"	*NEANISKOS*
Isaiah 40:30	"young men"	*NEANISKOS*
Isaiah 42:22	Not translated	Not translated
Isaiah 62:5	"young man"	*NEANISKOS*
Jeremiah 6:11	"young men"	*NEANISKOS*
Jeremiah 9:21	"young men"	*NEANISKOS*
Jeremiah 11:22	"young men"	*NEANISKOS*
Jeremiah 15:8	"young men"	*NEANISKOS*
Jeremiah 18:21	"young men"	*NEANISKOS*
Jeremiah 31:13	"young men"	*NEANISKOS*
Jeremiah 48:15	"young men"	*NEANISKOS*
Jeremiah 49:26	"young men"	*NEANISKOS*
Jeremiah 50:30	"young men"	*NEANISKOS*
Jeremiah 51:3	"young men"	*NEANISKOS*
Jeremiah 51:22	"young man"	*NEANISKOS*
Lamentations 1:15	**"young men"**	***EKLEKTOS***

Lamentations 1:18	"young men"	*NEANISKOS*
Lamentations 2:21	"young men"	*NEANISKOS*
Lamentations 5:13	**"young men"**	***EKLEKTOS***
Lamentations 5:14	**"young men"**	***EKLEKTOS***
Ezekiel 9:6	"young"	*NEANISKOS*
Ezekiel 23:6	"young men"	*NEANISKOS*
Ezekiel 23:12	"young men"	*NEANISKOS*
Ezekiel 23:23	"young men"	*NEANISKOS*
Ezekiel 30:17	"young men"	*NEANISKOS*
Joel 2:28	"young men"	*NEANISKOS*
Amos 2:11	"young men"	*NEANISKOS*
Amos 4:10	"young men"	*NEANISKOS*
Amos 8:13	"young men"	*NEANISKOS*
Zechariah 9:17	"young men"	*NEANISKOS*

Is "chosen" in Psalm 78:31 in the KJV part of a pattern for BACHUR?
No.

Could it even be called a rogue example, even in the KJV?
Yes.

Thus, it is reasonable to remove BACHUR as a doubt to the meaning of *EKLEKTOS* as "excellent", "top quality": A young man in the setting of the OT was as prime soldier material: excellent.

BARAR

The meaning for BARAR under the heading seen in the preceding chapter is:

"**pure** . . . **pure**" – pure, choice, clean

Robert Young in his Analytical Concordance places BARAR under "to purify" (page 165).

In English, the main renderings for this Hebrew word across the KJV are:

97

"pure" 5, "choice" 2, "clean" 2, "clearly" 1, "manifest" 1, "bright" 1, "Purge out" 1, "polished" 1, "purge" 1 and, "purified" 1.

The exception is: "chosen" 2.

These are 1 Chronicles 9:22 "**chosen** as gatekeepers" and, 1 Chronicles 16:41 "Heman and Jeduthun, and the rest who were **chosen**, who were designated by name".

1 Chronicles 9:22 is translated in the LXX by *EKLEKTOS* and 1 Chronicles 16:41 by *EKLEGÓ* (to choose) which, as a verb also occurs for BARAR in Ezekiel 20:38 which in English is rendered as "**I will purge the rebels from among you**". So this is a total (exception) of three occasions.

The main emphasis of "to purify" to "be clean" shows us that any actual choosing is not independent of the chosen having been made clean or involved in being purged. Without a cleaning, a purging or purifying involved, this word is not involved.

Here they are in English:

1 Chronicles 9:22 BARAR – LXX *EKLEKTOS*

> All those **chosen** as gatekeepers *were* two hundred and twelve. They were recorded by their genealogy, in their villages. David and Samuel the seer had appointed them to their trusted office.

1 Chronicles 16:41 BARAR – LXX *EKLEGÓ*

> and with them Heman and Jeduthun and the rest who were **chosen**, who were designated by name, to give thanks to the LORD, because His mercy *endures* forever;

Ezekiel 20:38 BARAR – LXX *EKLEGÓ*

> I **will purge** the rebels from among you, and those who transgress against Me; I will bring them out of the country where they sojourn, but they shall not enter the land of Israel. Then you will know that I *am* the LORD.

We can see that "purified", "cleansed" and "to purge" are good alternatives to place here, in line with the main emphasis for BARAR. So that there is no independent element of choice (a choosing) made here irrespective of any cleaning, purifying or purging action being present.

Can BARAR thereby be seen as a reasonable doubt to see *EKLEKTOS* as about top quality, excellent?
No.

And, that since it always involves removing non top quality elements before being picked or chosen.

MIBCHAR

The meaning for MIBCHAR under the heading in the preceding chapter is:

"the **choicest** of our burial places" – choice, choicest

In English, the main renderings for this Hebrew word across the KJV are:
"choice" 7 and, "choicest" 1.

The exception is: "chosen" 4.

The 4 are:
Jeremiah 48:15 and Daniel 11:15 translated in the LXX by *EKLEKTOS* and then there are two given by *EPILEKTOS*[1] in the LXX at Exodus 15:4 and Ezekiel 23:7 ([1]see also next chapter)

Other translators than the KJV are as follows
For all 4 passages in order:

Exodus 15:4 MIBCHAR – LXX *EPILEKTOS*

Pharaoh's chariots and his army He has cast into the sea; his **chosen** captains also are drowned in the Red Sea.

Pharaoh's chariots and his host hath he cast into the sea: his

chosen captains also are drowned in the Red sea.   *KJV*

Chariots of Pharaoh and his force He hath cast into the sea;
and the **choice** of his captains have sunk in the Red Sea!
                                                    YLT

"Pharaoh's chariots and his army He has cast into the sea;
and the **choicest** of his officers are drowned in the Red Sea.
                                                    NASB

Pharaoh's chariots and his army he has hurled into the sea.
The **best** of Pharaoh's officers are drowned in the Red Sea.
                                                    NIV

Pharaoh's chariots and army he has hurled into the sea. The
finest of Pharaoh's officers are drowned in the Red Sea.
                                                    NLT

LXX

HARMATA PHARAÓ KAI TÉN DUNAMIN AUTOU
  chariots of Pharaoh and the   power   of him

ERRHIPSEN EIS THALASSAN
  tossed   into   sea

EPILEKTOUS *ANABATAS TRISTATAS KATEPOTHÉSAN*
  choice   mounted   officers   sank

EN ERUTHRA THALASSÉ
 in   red   sea

engLXX
He has cast the chariots of Pharao and his host into the sea, the chosen
mounted captains: they were swallowed up in the Red Sea.

Jeremiah 48:15 MIBCHAR – LXX *EKLEKTOS*

Moab is plundered and gone up *from* her cities; her **chosen**
young men have gone down to the slaughter," says the King,
whose name *is* the LORD of hosts.

Moab is spoiled, and gone up *out of* her cities, and his

chosen young men are gone down to the slaughter, saith the King, whose name *is* the LORD of hosts.   *KJV*

Spoiled is Moab, and her cities hath one gone up, and the **choice** of its young men have gone down to slaughter, an affirmation of the King, Jehovah of Hosts *is* His name.   *YLT*

"Moab has been destroyed and men have gone up to his cities; his **choicest** young men have also gone down to the slaughter," declares the King, whose name is the LORD of hosts.   *NASB*

Moab will be destroyed and her towns invaded; her **finest** young men will go down in the slaughter,' declares the King, whose name is the LORD Almighty.   *NIV*

But now Moab and his towns will be destroyed. His **most promising** youth are doomed to slaughter," says the King, whose name is the LORD of Heaven's Armies.   *NLT*

LXX 31:15

[See DEiTB for the list of differences between the placements of passages in Jeremiah]

*ÓLETO MÓAB POLIS AUTOU KAI **EKLEKTOI***
destroyed Moab cities   of it and   choice

NEANISKOI AUTOU KATEBÉSAN EIS SPHAGÉN
 young men of him   went down to slaughter

engLXX
Moab is ruined, *even* his city, and his choice young men have gone down to slaughter.

Ezekiel 23:7 MIBCHAR – LXX *EPILEKTOS*

Thus she committed her harlotry with them, all of them **choice** men of Assyria; and with all for whom she lusted, with all their idols, she defiled herself.

Thus she committed her whoredoms with them, with all them *that were* the **chosen** men of Assyria, and with all on whom she doted: with all their idols she defiled herself. *KJV*

And she giveth her whoredoms on them, the **choice** of the sons of Asshur, all of them - even all on whom she doted, by all their idols she hath been defiled. *YLT*

She bestowed her harlotries on them, all of whom *were* the **choicest** men of Assyria; and with all whom she lusted after, with all their idols she defiled herself. *NASB*

She gave herself as a prostitute to all the **elite** of the Assyrians and defiled herself with all the idols of everyone she lusted after. *NIV*

And so she prostituted herself with the **most desirable** men of Assyria, worshiping their idols and defiling herself. *NLT*

LXX

KAI EDÓKE TÉN PORNEIAN AUTÉS EP AUTOUS
and   gave   the whoredoms of her upon them

***EPILEKTOI** HUIOI ASSURIÓN PANTES KAI EPI PANTAS*
    choice   sons of Assyrians   all   and upon   all

HOUS EPETHETO EN PASI TOIS ENTHUMÉMASIN
whom   doted   in   all the   thoughts

AUTOIS EMIAINETO
to them   defile

engLXX

And she bestowed her fornication upon them; all were choice sons of the Assyrians: and on whomsoever she doted herself, with them she defiled herself in all *their* devices.

Daniel 11:15 MIBCHAR – LXX EKLEKTOS

"So the king of the North shall come and build a siege mound, and take a fortified city; and the forces of the South shall not withstand *him*. Even his **choice** troops *shall have* no strength to resist.

So the king of the north shall come, and cast up a mount, and take the most fenced cities: and the arms of the south shall not withstand, neither his **chosen** people, neither *shall there be any* strength to withstand. *KJV*

And the king of the north cometh in, and poureth out a mount, and hath captured fenced cities; and the arms of the south do not stand, nor the people of his **choice**, yea, there is no power to stand. *YLT*

Then the king of the North will come, cast up a siege ramp and capture a well-fortified city; and the forces of the South will not stand *their ground*, not even their **choicest** troops, for there will be no strength to make a stand. *NASB*

Then the king of the North will come and build up siege ramps and will capture a fortified city. The forces of the South will be powerless to resist; even their **best** troops will not have the strength to stand. *NIV*

Then the king of the north will come and lay siege to a fortified city and capture it. The **best** troops of the south will not be able to stand in the face of the onslaught. *NLT*

LXX

KAI EISELEUSETAI BASILEUS TOU BORRHA KAI
and   enter   king   of the north and

EKCHEEI PROSCHÓMA KAI SULLÉPSETAI POLEIS
pour out   mounds   and   seize   cities

OCHURAS KAI HOI BRACHIONES TOU BASILEÓS TOU
strong and the   arms   of the king of the

NOTOU STÉSONTAI KAI ANASTÉSONTAI HOI
south   stand and   arise   the

EKLEKTOI *AUTOU KAI OUK ESTAI ISCHUS TOU STÉNAI*
choice   of him and not shall be strength of the to stand

engLXX

> And the king of the north shall come in, and cast up a mound,
> and take strong cities: and the arms of the king of the south
> shall withstand, and his chosen ones shall rise up, but there
> shall be no strength to stand.

With this range of understanding for MIBCHAR in English, in every place it is found – the 4 examples above being only the "doubt" locations - and, in each of these, various translations hold to the top quality meaning, is there a reasonable doubt that MIBCHAR can in itself mean "to choose" or "chosen"?
Yes.

MIBCHAR then, can only thereby be used to show *EKLEKTOS* as about "top quality, excellent"

_____

_____

With the four words BACHAR, BACHUR, BARAR and MIBCHAR not fit to be used as a reasonable doubt, as evidently seen, there then exists no more objection to the meaning of "top quality, excellent" for *EKLEKTOS* anywhere in the LXX.

Other historical pointers

EPILEKTOS

In the preceding chapter we saw how MIBCHAR, without a reasonable doubt, stood for top "quality, excellent, choice". We also saw it translated in the LXX by *EPILEKTOS*, a word not found in the NT.

EPILEKTOS is a Greek word in the same family as *EKLEKTOS*.
EK is the preposition for "from" or "out of" and, *EPI* is the preposition for "on" or "upon".

Our English equivalent of *EK* is "ex" which we see in words like "excessive", "extraordinary", "excellent". It gives an "extra" or "extreme" outward or highest element of emphasis.

The root of *EPILEKTOS* and *EKLEKTOS* is "*-LEKTOS*" and differs from another family of words which also uses the same two prepositions *EK* and *EPI*, but uses the root "*-LEGÓ*". This shows thereby that *EKLEKTOS* is not related to that category: *EKLEGÓ* and *EPILEGÓ*. See BACHAR in the preceding chapter for the main use of BACHAR with *EKLEGÓ* and *EPILEGÓ* included.

This means all lexicons suggesting a family link between *EKLEKTOS* and *EKLEGÓ* or, *EKLEKTOS* and *EKLEGOMAI*: these are incorrect.

The flavour of *EPI* as in "higher" or, "over" or, "highest" is seen in the examples below.

List of EPILEKTOS in the LXX	From Hebrew word	Meaning
Exodus 15:4	[1]MIBCHAR	choice, top quality
	([1]See previous chapter)	
Exodus 24:11	ATSILIM	chief men (1) nobles (1)
Joshua 17:16	NOT From Heb.	N/A
Joshua 17:18	NOT From Heb.	N/A

Ezekiel 17:3	TSAMMERETH	highest branch (2) top (1)
Ezekiel 23:6	CHEMED	Young: desirable (3) pleasant (2) [CHEMER red wine 1 pure 1] Strong: Desirable 3 Pleasant 2 [of red wine 1]
Ezekiel 23:7	MIBCHAR	choice, top quality (see above)
Ezekiel 23:12	CHEMED	See Ezekiel 23:6
Ezekiel 23:23	CHEMED	See Ezekiel 23:6
Ezekiel 24:5	MIBCHAR	choice, top quality (see[1] above)
Joel 3:5	MACHMAD	pleasant thing (4) desire (3) beloved fruit (1) pleasant place (1) goodly (1) lovely (1) pleasant (1)

CLEMENT of Rome's LETTER

At the end of the 1st century, Clement is seen as one of the first senior bishops of Rome. Clement wrote a letter on behalf of the Rome leadership to the church at Corinth. We find this letter in the Greek of the NT. In this letter it is reasonable to see his use of the word *EKLEKTOS* just like the New Testament and also just like the LXX.

It is of note: Clement wrote his letter, not on his own authority, but that of the team for whom he spoke and indeed for the whole church at Rome. This can be seen from his use of the plural pronouns "we" and "us", at the beginning,

> By reason of the sudden and repeated calamities and reverses which are befalling us, brethren, we consider that we have been somewhat tardy in giving heed to the matters of dispute that have arisen among you, dearly beloved

1 Clement 1:1

At the end,

> **For ye will give us great joy and gladness, if ye render obedience**
> **unto the things written by us through the Holy Spirit, and**
> **root out the unrighteous anger of your jealousy, according**
> **to the entreaty which we have made for peace and concord**
> **in this letter**   *1 Clement 63:2*

And, at the middle, in saying how new leaders should be appointed
by Corinth, in the following manner, it testifies well that this was the
process already in place at Rome too:

> **with the consent of the whole Church**   *1 Clement 44:2*

This was not a letter with authority over another, but a letter of support
and entreaty from brothers to brothers.

Clement quotes a portion of Samuel – I quote here the translation
from the Hebrew into Eng.

> **With the merciful You will show Yourself merciful; with a**
> **blameless man You will show Yourself blameless; with the**
> **pure You will show Yourself pure; and with the devious You**
> **will show Yourself shrewd.**   *2 Samuel 22:26-27*

The portion of Scripture Clement quotes, since he wrote in Greek, is
word for word identical to the LXX:

> *. . . KAI META* **EKLEKTOU EKLEKTOS** *ESÉ KAI META*
> *STEBLOU . . .*   *1 Clement 46:3*

This has been translated directly (note the word "elect" assumed by the
later translator) as:

> … and with the elect thou shalt be elect, and with the crooked …
>   *1 Clement 46:3*

We saw how BARAR with the word "pure" in the Hebrew "**with the**
pure You will show Yourself pure" is in the LXX by *EKLEKTOS*. We
saw in the preceding chapter top quality is the emphasis here for this
Greek word. We can see this is also Clement's reading and the way he

uses the Greek word *EKLEKTOS* because of the progression of thought that is readable in his letter:

> **But they that endured patiently in confidence inherited glory and honor; they were exalted, and had their names recorded by God in their memorial for ever and ever. Amen.**
>
> *1 Clement 45:8*
>
> **To such examples as these therefore, brethren, we also ought to cleave.** *1 Clement 46:1*
>
> **For it is written; Cleave unto the saints, for they that cleave unto them shall be sanctified.** *1 Clement 46:2*
>
> **And again He saith in another place; With the guiltless man thou shalt be guiltless, and with the *EKLEKTOU* thou shalt be *EKLEKTOS*, and with the crooked thou shalt deal crookedly.**
>
> *1 Clement 46:3*

Clement shares in 45:8 about saints who "**endured patiently**". In 46:1 he mentions these guys are an example to stick to. In 46:2 he says that to those who stick to this example for themselves, there is a reward of sanctification. Then in 46:3 he quotes the Scripture to prove his point that those who act as saints are treated as saints by God and, conversely, those who do wickedly are treated as sinners.

So, Clement's use of *EKLEKTOS* in this passage is to emphasise quality: righteous living in contrast to wickedness. The flow of meaning involves being good, as per the preceding example of those who "**endured patiently**" and, in doing so, there is a corresponding reward from God. There is no implication of a selection involved: "elect" and anything like "selected" or "chosen by God" as a meaning is excluded from the flow of thought portrayed to us by Clement in the letter.

Clement then seals off the quality emphasis with:

> **Let us therefore cleave to the guiltless and righteous: and these are the *EKLEKTOI* of God.** *1 Clement 46:4*

Following in his flow about quality, here Clement is explicit in describing someone *EKLEKTOS*: it is all those who equally exemplify the guiltless and righteous: no inference of a decision of God in the process, but only of the individual living righteously. It is the excellent: the guiltless and righteous.

It is reasonable to see then that - with the Ecumenical Council of Nicea in 325AD which was conducted and recorded in Greek - we know the whole Christian world, for the first full three centuries, read *EKLEKTOS* with the idea of "best, top quality, excellent" in their OT bible and in their NT letters and gospels.

ROBERT YOUNG

A revision and correction of lexicons is in order.

One bible translator who did his own research of every word in Hebrew and every word in Greek that make up the bible's first languages also came to this decision in regards to *EKLEKTOS*: his name is Robert Young. He produced his own analytical concordance (1879) and his own literal rendering of the bible (the YLT – 1862).

For "**elect**" the recommendation Young gives, is to think "**(read) 'choice one'** " – he gives this in an Explanation of Bible Terms: a list of 100 bible terms in the introduction to the NT - and indeed, he goes further by translating it that very way also in a number of places.

For example his rendering of 1 Peter 1:1

> "**Peter, an apostle of Jesus Christ, to the choice [*EKLEKTOS*] sojourners of the dispersion of Pontus, Galatia, Cappadocia, Asia, and Bithynia, according to a fore-knowledge of God the Father, in sanctification of the Spirit, to obedience and sprinkling of the blood of Jesus Christ: Grace to you and peace be multiplied!**"   *1 Peter 1:1-2 YLT*

This is a world apart from:

> "**Peter, an apostle of Jesus Christ, to the strangers scattered throughout Pontus, Galatia, Cappadocia, Asia, and Bithynia, Elect [*EKLEKTOS*] according to the foreknowledge of God the Father, through sanctification of the Spirit, unto obedience and sprinkling of the blood of Jesus Christ: Grace unto you, and peace, be multiplied.**"   *1 Peter 1:1-2 KJV*

Also note the re-arrangement of the words in the KJV to give an emphasis not seen in the Greek: A re-arrangement which has been repeated in other versions like the NKJV and the NASB. It is good to see the arrangement is correct in the NIV and the NLT.

Here is a simple Greek – English interlinear with the same Greek text as the KJV, NKJV and YLT showing the YLT follows the arrangement well.

1 Peter 1:1-2 Greek RT - The Received Text

PETROS APOSTOLOS IÉSOU CHRISTOU **EKLEKTOIS**
Peter   apostle   of Jesus   Christ   to choice

PAREPIDÉMOIS DIASPORAS PONTOU GALATIAS
sojourners   of dispersion of Pontus   Galatia

KAPPADOKIAS ASIAS KAI BITHUNIAS KATA
Cappadocia   Asia   and   Bithynia according to

PROGNÓSIN THEOU PATROS EN HAGIASMÓ PNEUMATOS
foreknowledge of God Father in   holy-ing   of Spirit

EIS HUPAKOÉN KAI RHANTISMON HAIMATOS
into   obedience and   sprinkling   of blood

IÉSOU CHRISTOU CHARIS HUMIN KAI EIRÉNÉ
of Jesus   Christ   Grace   to you   and   peace

PLÉTHUNTHEIÉ
be multiplied

[See also next chapter for this passage]

So how should we translate
BACHIR and *EKLEKTOS*?

From the English translating the Hebrew words that *EKLEKTOS* was rendering in the LXX we saw the following:

In the chapter with just one example from each of the 23 Hebrew words:

MIBCHAR (**choicest**), BARI (**fat**), DEROR (**liquid/pure** myrrh KJV), BECHURIM/BECHUROTH (**choice men/young men** KJV), BARAR (**pure + pure**), BACHUR (**young men**), MIBCHOR (**choice**), GELAL (**heavy** stones), MANAMMIM (**delicacies**), BACHAR (**choice** silver), CHARUTS (**diligent**), BAR (**favourite/choice** KJV/**pure** *child* NASB), NESHEQ (**armor** of the House), BO-CHAN (**tried** stone), CHEPHETS (**precious** stones), CHEMDAH/CHAMUDOTH (**pleasant** land), MATSOR (**fortress/bulwark** YLT), TSEBI (**beauty**), TSAMMERETH (**highest branches**), PERI (**fruit**), CHOPHESH (**saddlecloths/precious** clothes KJV), BEROMIM (**multicolored apparel**), MASETH (**taxes/ burdens** of wheat KJV).

In the expanding chapter of those without seeming "doubt", these were then added:
BAR ("**clear/pure** NASB/**bright** as the sun NIV"), BARI ("**fatted** oxen", "food **plentious**", "**plump**" two times &, "**fat**" a further 4 times), CHEMDAH/CHAMUDOTH ("**precious** vessel", "**Desire** of All Nations", "**pleasant** land"), PERI ("**fruit**" 1 more time), TSEBI ("**glory** of the country").

The definition of an anomaly is:
"something that deviates from what is standard, normal, or expected."

We saw that the use of "chosen" for rendering BACHAR, BACHUR, BARAR and MIBCHAR in English was an anomaly in all the passages where it was rendered by *EKLEKTOS* in the LXX.

So that all the "top quality" examples for these four Hebrew words are now added:

BACHAR:
"**choice** chariots", "**select** chariots - NASB", "**best** chariots - NIV, NLT", "**choice** men - NASB" 2 times, "**select** men" 2 times, "**able young** men - NIV" 3 times, "**elite troops** - NLT" 4 times, "**select** . . . **troops** - NIV", "**a young man** - NIV", "**excellent** as the cedars", "**choice** . . . cedars - NASB, NIV", "**noble** cedars - NLT"

BACHUR:
BACHUR: "**choice** *men*" + "**young men**" 3 more times/**young warriors** NLT

BARAR:
("**pure**" 2 more times, "**choice men**, mighty men of valor", "**choice** sheep", "a **polished** shaft", "**select men** NLT" and, "a **polished** shaft/**select** arrow NASB/**polished** arrow NIV/**sharp** arrow NLT")

BARAR: ("**pure**" 2 more times, "**choice men**, mighty men of valor", "**choice** sheep", "a **polished** shaft", "**select men** NLT" and, "a **polished** shaft/**select** arrow NASB/**polished** arrow NIV/**sharp** arrow NLT")

MIBCHAR:
"**choice** (offerings)", "**choicest** valleys/**beautiful** valleys NLT" X2, "**choicest** young men NASB/**finest** young men NIV/**most promising** youth NLT", "the **choice** and best/the **choicest** and best NASB, NIV/the **most beautiful** NLT" and, "**choice** troops/their **choicest** troops NASB/the **best** troops NIV, NLT"

All these English meanings, since they are rendered by *EKLEKTOS* in the LXX, are helpful to give us a good picture of the ways we can now re-align the passages where we find BACHIR in the OT and *EKLEKTOS* in the NT.

Remember,
For about 3 centuries Christians coming across the word *EKLEKTOS* only saw the meaning of "excellent, the best".

The Old Testament they read was in Greek, the LXX, and

there all translations of the Hebrew BACHIR were found rendered by *EKLEKTOS*.

Today, in most bibles (i.e. excluding the YLT mostly) you find "**elect**" or "**chosen**" rendered for either of those two words.

So with the early Christians only seeing the one word *EKLEKTOS*, what should we be reading in each of the passages for BACHIR and for *EKLEKTOS*?

Well, if the definite article "**The**" is tied to either of these source words anything like:

"**The excellent**", "**The best**", "**The finest**", "**The superior**", "**The outstanding**", "**The exceptional**"

These are literal renderings for "the" *EKLEKTOS* and "the" BACHIR.

This sudden "change" in place of the repeated "chosen" and "elect" for BACHIR and *EKLEKTOS*, though literally correct, may not however help a number of people too familiar with the older (incorrect) translation. In such a condition the following could be considered as suitable alternatives, though they are in themselves the direct translation of other Hebrew and Greek words: The meaning of high quality is still there, far better seen, than the meaning of "selected/chosen/elect" which is foreign and has been the mistranslation:

"**The good guys**", "**The righteous**", "**The faithful**", "**The saints**", "**The steadfast**"

In these the meaning is still seen with a high quality emphasis and is perhaps more easily understandable than the literal, until such a time that is, as the affected passages are familiar in their return to their proper use. For the OT passages I have gone more for the literal; for the NT passages I have gone more for the less literal, but provided extra explanation of thinking.

So let's look at a better translation for the 13 OT and 23 NT passages affected.

Here is the OT list followed by the word found in the KJV:

2 Samuel 21:6	BACHIR	choose
1 Chronicles 16:13	BACHIR	chosen
Psalm 89:3	BACHIR	chosen
Psalm 105:6	BACHIR	chosen
Psalm 105:43	BACHIR	chosen
Psalm 106:5	BACHIR	chosen
Psalm 106:23	BACHIR	chosen
Isaiah 42:1	BACHIR	elect
Isaiah 43:20	BACHIR	chosen
Isaiah 45:4	BACHIR	elect
Isaiah 65:9	BACHIR	elect
Isaiah 65:15	BACHIR	chosen
Isaiah 65:22	BACHIR	elect

2 Samuel 21:6
Where we find,

> "let seven men of his descendants be delivered to us, and we will hang them before the Lord in Gibeah of Saul, *whom* the Lord chose." And the king said, "I will give *them*."
>
> *2 Samuel 21:6*

Here it is in Young's literal with a closer order of words:

> 'let there be given to us seven men of his sons, and we have hanged them before Jehovah, in the height of Saul, the chosen of Jehovah.' And the king saith, 'I do give;'
>
> *2 Samuel 21:6 YLT*

this then reads,

> "Let there be given to us seven men of his sons, and we will hang them before the Lord, in Gibeah of Saul, the fit of the Lord." And the king said, "I will give them." *2 Samuel 21:6 JM*

In my chapter on BACHIR entitled "How did the first Christians read these passages? BACHIR and *EKLEKTOS*" the Greek declension for *EKLEKTOS* in this passage can be seen as *EKLEKTOUS*. This is in the plural meaning that the choice guys in view were the seven men, the descendants of Saul which were seen as the ones suitable and fit to be sacrificed as such. Being "fit" is a more modern use of the English word, representing someone as good looking or physically well trimmed and in good physique; I use it here to mean perfectly suitable to be sacrificed.

1 Chronicles 16:13

Here, we find,

> O seed of Israel His servant,
> You children of Jacob, His chosen ones!   *1 Chronicles 16:13*

The children of Israel are in view and, to God the seed of Israel is choice, previously named Jacob, but it is of note that the prophets kept mentioning how if any wicked were found in the midst, they were removed, thus retaining excellence in the remaining seed.

> O seed of Israel, His servant, O sons of Jacob, His finest!
> *1 Chronicles 16:13 JM*

Psalm 89:3

Here we find,

> I have made a covenant with My chosen, I have sworn to My
> servant David: *Psalm 89:3*

As per Verse 4 God deemed David highly "**Your seed I will establish forever, and build up your throne to all generations**", a man after His own heart (1 Samuel 13:14): excellent David.

> I have made a covenant with My best, I have sworn to David
> My servant: *Psalm 89:3 JM*

Psalm 105:6

Here we read,

> O seed of Abraham His servant, you children of Jacob, His
> chosen ones!   *Psalm 105:6*

Abraham is in view as the "servant" - to God the seed of Jacob is choice, but it is of note that the prophets kept mentioning how if any wicked were found in the midst, they were removed, thus retaining excellence in the remaining seed.

> **O seed of Abraham, His servant, O sons of Jacob, His finest!**
> *Psalm 105:6 JM*

Psalm 105:43
Here is,

> **He brought out His people with joy, His chosen ones with gladness.** *Psalm 105:43*

In Exodus 15:20-21 (NKJV) we read of this joy as God brought deliverance and led the people out of Egypt, "**Miriam the prophetess, the sister of Aaron, took the timbrel in her hand; and all the women went out after her with timbrels and with dances. And Miriam answered them: 'Sing to the LORD, for He has triumphed gloriously! The horse and its rider He has thrown into the sea!' **": a time of much rejoicing. Miriam is one of those identified alongside Moses and Aaron as choice: e.g. as per Micah 6:4 (NKJV) "**For I brought you up from the land of Egypt, I redeemed you from the house of bondage; and I sent before you Moses, Aaron, and Miriam.**" – These three rejoiced with Israel. To God the seed of Jacob is choice, but it is of note that the prophets kept mentioning how if any wicked were found in the midst, they were removed, thus retaining excellence in the remaining seed. This becomes,

> **And He brought out His people with joy, with jubilation His best ones.** *Psalm 105:43 JM*

Psalm 106:5
This reads,

> That I may see the benefit of Your chosen ones,
> That I may rejoice in the gladness of Your nation,
> That I may glory with Your inheritance. *Psalm 106:5*

Here is the YLT,

> To look on the good of Thy chosen ones,
> To rejoice in the joy of Thy nation,

> To boast myself with Thine inheritance.　　*Psalm 106:5 YLT*

The nation of Israel is choice before the Lord and is limited in blessing in the good and the rejoicing to the righteous as per the Lord's direct covenant with the nation (see Deuteronomy 30) and the specific context "**O the happiness of those keeping judgment, doing righteousness at all times.**" (Psalm 106:3 YLT). This is now,

> **To look on the good of Your best ones, to rejoice in the joy of Your nation, to boast myself with Your inheritance.**
>
> *Psalm 106:5 JM*

Psalm 106:23

Here we see,

> **Therefore He said that He would destroy them, had not Moses His chosen one stood before Him in the breach, to turn away His wrath, lest He destroy *them*.**

Moses was mentioned as "**the man Moses *is* very humble, more than any of the men who *are* on the face of the ground**" (Numbers 12:3 YLT) and Jesus said "**whoever humbles himself as this little child is the greatest in the kingdom of heaven**" (Matthew 18:4) so, we know Moses as excellent in God's eyes: choice.

> **And He said that He would destroy them, had not Moses His excellent one stood before Him in the breach, to turn away His wrath, lest He destroy.**　　*Psalm 106:23 JM*

Isaiah 42:1

Here we find,

> **"Behold! My Servant whom I uphold, My Elect One *in whom* My soul delights!**
> **I have put My Spirit upon Him; He will bring forth justice to the Gentiles.**　　*Isaiah 42:1*

A prophetic word about the coming Messiah: Jesus e.g. "**a light to the Gentiles**" (Verse 6) fulfilled in "**A light to *bring* revelation to the Gentiles**" (Luke 2:32) – As this is about the Eternal Son of God: God manifest in the flesh (1 Timothy 3:16 KJV/NKJV/YLT – quoted by

Ignatius of Antioch 1st century AD Magnesians 8:2, et al), He is not chosen or picked out, but is the Excellent One, the Choice One. This becomes,

> "Look! My Servant whom I uphold, My Excellent One My soul delights!
> I have put My Spirit upon Him; He will bring forth justice to the Gentiles.
> *Isaiah 42:1 JM*

Isaiah 43:20

We read,

> The beast of the field will honor Me, the jackals and the ostriches, because I give waters in the wilderness *and* rivers in the desert, to give drink to My people, My chosen.
> *Isaiah 43:20*

To God His people, the seed of Israel is choice "This people I have formed for Myself, My praise they recount." (Verse 21 YLT), but it is of note that the prophet mentions how the wicked are judged (Verses 22-28), they are removed, thus retaining excellence in the remaining seed: a choice people: excellent. This is now rendered,

> The beast of the field will honour Me, the jackals and the ostriches, because I give waters in the wilderness *and* rivers in the desert, to give drink to My people, My best.
> *Isaiah 43:20 JM*

Isaiah 45:4

We find,

> For Jacob My servant's sake, and Israel My elect, I have even called you by your name; I have named you, though you have not known Me.
> *Isaiah 45:4*

Jacob was renamed Israel after his wrestling match: The Lord said "Thy name is no more called Jacob, but Israel; for thou hast been a prince with God and with men, and dost prevail" (Genesis 32:28 YLT) so, it was due to his excellence in prevailing that he was considered excellent. This now reads,

> For Jacob My servant's sake, and Israel My excellent, I have
> even called you by your name; I have named you, though
> you have not known Me. *Isaiah 45:4 JM*

Isaiah 65:9

Reads,

> I will bring forth descendants from Jacob, and from Judah
> an heir of My mountains; My elect shall inherit it, and My
> servants shall dwell there. *Isaiah 65:9*

Following the express retaining of the few from the many (see Verse
8), following much testing and purifying, the remainder will be the
choice. This then is,

> I will bring forth descendants from Jacob, and from Judah
> an heir of My mountains; My excellent ones shall inherit it,
> and My servants shall dwell there. *Isaiah 65:9*

Isaiah 65:15

We see,

> You shall leave your name as a curse to My chosen; for the
> Lord GOD will slay you, and call His servants by another
> name; *Isaiah 65:15*

The wicked and unbelieving in the midst of Israel Verses 11-12 shames
all of Israel so that, at the end, what the faithful are named by, will be
different: these faithful are the choice in view in contrast to the
unfaithful. This then reads,

> You shall leave your name as a curse to My excellent ones;
> for the Lord God will slay you, and call His servants by
> another name; *Isaiah 65:15 JM*

Isaiah 65:22

Reads,

> They shall not build and another inhabit; they shall not
> plant and another eat; for as the days of a tree, *so shall be* the

days of My people, and My elect shall long enjoy the work of their hands. *Isaiah 65:22*

The remaining people, faithful and true, are choice [see Verses 9 and 15 above]. This becomes,

They shall not build and another inhabit; they shall not plant and another eat; for as the days of a tree, the days of My people, and My excellent shall long enjoy the work of their hands. *Isaiah 65:22 JM*

The NT list followed by the word found in the KJV:

Matthew 20:16[1]	*EKLEKTOS*	chosen
Matthew 22:14	*EKLEKTOS*	chosen
Matthew 24:22	*EKLEKTOS*	elect
Matthew 24:24	*EKLEKTOS*	elect
Matthew 24:31	*EKLEKTOS*	elect
Mark 13:20	*EKLEKTOS*	elect
Mark 13:22	*EKLEKTOS*	elect
Mark 13:27	*EKLEKTOS*	elect
Luke 18:7	*EKLEKTOS*	elect
Luke 23:35	*EKLEKTOS*	chosen
Romans 8:33	*EKLEKTOS*	elect
Romans 16:13	*EKLEKTOS*	chosen
Colossians 3:12	*EKLEKTOS*	elect
1 Timothy 5:21	*EKLEKTOS*	elect
2 Timothy 2:10	*EKLEKTOS*	elect
Titus 1:1	*EKLEKTOS*	elect
1 Peter 1:2(Gk. 1:1 & YLT)	*EKLEKTOS*	elect
1 Peter 2:4	*EKLEKTOS*	chosen
1 Peter 2:6	*EKLEKTOS*	elect
1 Peter 2:9	*EKLEKTOS*	chosen
2 John 1:1	*EKLEKTOS*	elect
2 John 1:13	*EKLEKTOS*	elect
Revelation 17:14	*EKLEKTOS*	chosen

[1]KJV, YLT, NKJV i.e. This set of words is found in the Received Text from which these

versions are translated. The source Greek text used by other translation omits them (See DEiTB).

Matthew 20:16

Where we find,

> . . . For many are called, but few chosen.   *Matthew 20:16*

this becomes.

> . . . For many are called, but few *have* mettle.
>
>   *Matthew 20:16 JM*

See note[1] above.

Matthew 22:14

Equally we find,

> For many are called, but few *are* chosen.   *Matthew 22:14*

this then is also,

> For many are called, but few *have* mettle. *Matthew 22:14 JM*

Matthew 24:22

Where we read,

> And unless those days were shortened, no flesh would be saved; but for the elect's sake those days will be shortened.
>
>   *Matthew 24:22*

this is more clearly understood with,

> And unless those days were shortened, no flesh would be saved; but for the righteous' sake those days will be shortened.   *Matthew 24:22 JM*

Matthew 24:24

Since "top quality" is better pictured in English with "the righteous" then with "the saints" I used it in Mark 13:20 (below), but here to help focus on the believing individuals involved "the saints" is suitable. Though neither the Greek words for "righteous" and "saints" are present, this rendering recognises the high quality element of *EKLEKTOS*; "the excellent" would be a literal rendering.

> For false Christs and false prophets will arise and show great signs and wonders, so as to deceive, if possible, even the elect.
> *Matthew 24:24*

This would then become,

> For false Christs and false prophets will arise and show great signs and wonders, so as to deceive, if possible, even the saints.
> *Matthew 24:24 JM*

Matthew 24:31

This use of "saints" in English is seen again like Matthew 24:24 as appropriate here, though "His righteous" or "His righteous ones" could work dependent on the desired flow of the translator:

> And He will send His angels with a great sound of a trumpet, and they will gather together His elect from the four winds, from one end of heaven to the other.
> *Matthew 24:31*

this then becomes,

> And He will send His angels with a great sound of a trumpet, and they will gather together His saints from the four winds, from one end of heaven to the other.
> *Matthew 24:31 JM*

Mark 13:20

This Mark prophecy is the same as in Matthew 24:22,

> And unless the Lord had shortened those days, no flesh would be saved; but for the elect's sake, whom He chose, He shortened the days.
> *Mark 13:20*

Now, since "chosen" and "elect" are interchangeable, a reason "elect" has been used here by the translator rather than "chosen" is that it would have been odd and strange looking to read "**for the chosen's sake, whom He chose**". If they are "chosen" then why repeat the fact? But, (since *EKLEKTOS* is about top quality – as is manifest historically – then the passage is about the good guys whom the Lord chose to go through those days. And it is for their sake that the days are shortened: the time is thus limited for them to be patient and endure the suffering season. So here we need,

> And unless the Lord had shortened those days, no flesh would be saved; but for the righteous' sake, whom He chose, He shortened the days.   *Mark 13:20 JM*

Mark 13:22

The thinking in Matthew 24:24 is valid for this parallel text.

> For false christs and false prophets will rise and show signs and wonders to deceive, if possible, even the elect.
>
> *Mark 13:22*

So, like Matthew 24:24 then becomes,

> For false christs and false prophets will rise and show signs and wonders to deceive, if possible, even the saints.
>
> *Mark 13:22 JM*

Mark 13:27

As per the parallel passage of Matthew 24:31 it is also here,

> And then He will send His angels, and gather together His elect from the four winds, from the farthest part of earth to the farthest part of heaven.   *Mark 13:27*

then becomes,

> And then He will send His angels, and gather together His saints from the four winds, from the farthest part of earth to the farthest part of heaven.   *Mark 13:27 JM*

Luke 18:7

Remember it is "top quality" that is the emphasis so any word that helps bring that out is useful and I use here "faithful" to show this,

> And shall God not avenge His own elect who cry out day and night to Him, though He bears long with them?   *Luke 18:7*

this then becomes,

> And shall God not avenge His own faithful who cry out day and night to Him, though He bears long with them?
>
> *Luke 18:7 JM*

Luke 23:35

Here in the sense of "the special one" the words "the anointed" serve sufficiently to remove a selection emphasis. Bearing in mind, this is a quoted sneer or sarcastic remark: it works to show the intended special-ness and uniqueness of Jesus,

> And the people stood looking on. But even the rulers with them sneered, saying, "He saved others; let Him save Himself if He is the Christ, the chosen of God." *Luke 23:35*

then becomes,

> And the people stood looking on. But even the rulers with them sneered, saying, "He saved others; let Him save Himself if He is the Christ, the Anointed of God." *Luke 23:35 JM*

The literal, "the Excellent", would work well here too.

Romans 8:33

Here in English the word "saints" or "faithful" serve well. Even though these, as mentioned above, are normally translations of their own separate Greek word counterparts. The "excellent" would be the literal rendering.

> Who shall bring a charge against God's elect? *It is* God who justifies.   *Romans 8:33*

This then becomes,

> Who shall bring a charge against God's saints? God *is* the righteous declarer.   *Romans 8:33 JM*

Romans 16:13

The same applies here as Romans 8:33,

> Greet Rufus, chosen in the Lord, and his mother and mine.
> *Romans 16:13*

this then becomes,

> Greet Rufus, faithful in the Lord, and his mother and mine.
> *Romans 16:13 JM*

Colossians 3:12

The same applies here as Romans 8:33,

> Therefore, as *the* elect of God, holy and beloved, put on tender mercies, kindness, humbleness of mind, meekness, longsuffering . . . *Colossians 3:12*

this then becomes,

> Therefore, as faithful of God, holy and beloved, put on tender mercies, kindness, humility, meekness, longsuffering . . . *Colossians 3:12 JM*

---

1 Timothy 5:21

Here a contrast is made between the two types of angels that exist: the fallen and wicked ones in contrast to those that remained at God's side from the beginning, so "good" ones as opposed to the "bad" ones serves well,

> I charge *you* before God and the Lord Jesus Christ and the elect angels that you observe these things without prejudice, doing nothing with partiality. *1 Timothy 5:21*

this then becomes,

> I testify fully before God and the Lord Jesus Christ and the good angels, that you observe these things without prejudice, doing nothing with partiality. *1 Timothy 5:21 JM*

---

2 Timothy 2:10

As we know from above top quality is the emphasis for *EKLEKTOS* and in view of the purpose Paul mentions in this verse I think it best to use "the righteous" more than "the saints" to translate *EKLEKTOS*, as the latter tends to be more used for those already Christians. And here when I read of "the righteous" I think of all, including those like Cornelius of whom Peter said "**In truth I perceive that God shows no partiality. But in every nation whoever fears Him and works righteousness is accepted by Him.**" (Acts 10:34-35). These then also need to hear the good news about Jesus that they may obtain assurance of salvation. So that the verse,

> Therefore I endure all things for the sake of the elect, that they also may obtain the salvation which is in Christ Jesus with eternal glory.   *2 Timothy 2:10*

then becomes,

> Therefore I endure all things for the sake of the righteous, that they also may obtain the salvation which is in Christ Jesus with eternal glory.   *2 Timothy 2:10 JM*

Titus 1:1

Here Paul introduces himself and his ministry to which he was called in sharing God's eternal purpose of everlasting life for the godly.

> Paul, a servant of God and an apostle of Jesus Christ, according to the faith of God's elect and the acknowledgment of the truth which is according to godliness, in hope of eternal life which God, who cannot lie, promised before time began . . .
>   *Titus 1:1-2*

In view of the truth relating to the godly or pious i.e. of all times, the righteous as opposed to the wicked, as two distinct groups are those seen throughout history in Scripture: the "righteous" emphasis then serves well more than "the saints" (cf. Romans 2:6-16).

> Paul, servant of God and apostle of Jesus Christ, according to the faith of God's righteous and knowledge of the truth which is according to piety upon hope of eternal life, which the un-lying God promised before the ages of time . . .
>   *Titus 1:1-2 JM*

---

1 Peter 1:1-2

Here it is helpful to note the order of the words in the Greek. A quick way to do that is quote Young's literal translation (See also preceding chapter where the Greek is quoted in full - Page 110):

> Peter, an apostle of Jesus Christ, to the choice sojourners of the dispersion of Pontus, Galatia, Cappadocia, Asia, and Bithynia, according to a foreknowledge of God the Father, in sanctification of the Spirit, to obedience and sprinkling

of the blood of Jesus Christ: Grace to you and peace be
multiplied! *1 Peter 1:1-2 YLT*

This helps take note of the deliberate re-ordering of the words apparent
to provide assistance to the idea of unconditional election as discussed
in the introductory chapter *The Challenge* and also see the preceding
chapter. The idea that there is an elect group – chosen and decided by
God is not in view in the text: But it appears that way when reading
"**elect according to the foreknowledge of God the Father**":

**Peter, an apostle of Jesus Christ, to the pilgrims of the
Dispersion in Pontus, Galatia, Cappadocia, Asia, and
Bithynia, elect according to the foreknowledge of God the
Father, in sanctification of the Spirit, for obedience and
sprinkling of the blood of Jesus Christ: Grace to you and
peace be multiplied.** *1 Peter 1:1-2*

If the actual order of the words are recognised and, that it is not needful
by manipulation to re-order them in order to assist any recognised
grammatical relationship, then all Peter is highlighting in the words
"**foreknowledge of God the Father, in sanctification of the Spirit,
to obedience and sprinkling of the blood of Jesus Christ**" is that
his introduction as an apostle and what that sending – an apostle is
someone "sent" – what this sending is about: the good news of salvation in
Jesus, the highlighted then is that gospel which was foreknown and is
part of his introduction in his letter:

To the question "What was foreknown?" the answer is: the
good news of the sanctification of the Spirit into obedience and
sprinkling of the blood of Jesus, i.e. the good news about Jesus of late
declared and at the core of his apostleship was foreknown, as was now
revealed at this time.

So as far as *EKLEKTOS* is concerned this passage has the "faithful" in
view and this is a good word to use.

**Peter, an apostle of Jesus Christ, to the faithful pilgrims of
the dispersion of Pontus, Galatia, Cappadocia, Asia, and
Bithynia, according to a foreknowledge of God the Father,
in sanctification of the Spirit, to obedience and sprinkling of**

> the blood of Jesus Christ: Grace to you and peace be multiplied!
>
> *1 Peter 1:1-2 JM*

---

1 Peter 2:4

Young's is useful here too in showing the quality meaning as it is self evident from the Person in view not being chosen from among others, but being the only begotten Son of God: Jesus.

> . . . to whom coming -- a living stone -- by men, indeed, having been disapproved of, but with God choice, precious . . .
>
> *1 Peter 2:4 YLT*

So that,

> Coming to Him *as to* a living stone, rejected indeed by men, but chosen by God and precious . . .   *1 Peter 2:4*

then becomes,

> Coming to Him, a living stone, rejected indeed by men, but with God fit, precious . . .   *1 Peter 2:4 JM*

"Tried" as in a "tried stone" also works well (see next verse). The ongoing challenge is to use an appropriate English word to show top quality which is the emphasis of the word as appropriate in the passage as it is a comparison between the worthlessness view in the rejection of men in contrast to the worthiness seen by God: a rejected stone by men, but one wholly fit for purpose to God.

---

1 Peter 2:6

This is a continuation of the theme in 1 Peter 2:4 and the same thinking applies. So that,

> Therefore it is also contained in the Scripture,
> *Behold, I lay in Zion a chief cornerstone, elect, precious, and he who believes on Him will by no means be put to shame.*
>
> *1 Peter 2:6*

The italics here are the practise of the NKJV version to show this is a quote from the OT:

> Therefore thus says the Lord GOD:

> "Behold, I lay in Zion a stone for a foundation, a tried stone, a precious cornerstone, a sure foundation; whoever believes will not act hastily."
> *Isaiah 28:16*

1 Peter 2:6 then becomes,

> *Behold, I lay in Zion a chief cornerstone, fit, precious, and he who believes on Him will by no means be put to shame.*
> *1 Peter 2:6 JM*

It is of note that no idea of selection: "chosen" or "elect" is to be found in the Old Testament Scripture whatsoever.

"Tried" would work too.

---

1 Peter 2:9

Continuing the theme that Jesus is special and top quality is seen in him, but now his followers are in view in contrast to unbelievers - those offended at Him, Peter here says that believers are not like these offended, but also are excellent like Jesus. Again Young shows this well.

> And ye *are* a choice race, a royal priesthood, a holy nation, a people acquired, that the excellences ye may shew forth of Him who out of darkness did call you to His wondrous light;
> *1 Peter 2:9 YLT*

So that this verse:

> But you *are* a chosen generation, a royal priesthood, a holy nation, His own special people, that you may proclaim the praises of Him who called you out of darkness into His marvellous light;
> *1 Peter 2:9*

Then becomes "**a choice race**" in Young: There is a choice as to what words are best to use to show the quality emphasis. As we see Young uses the word "choice" for quality and "race" rather than "generation" – see the chapter on *GENEA* in my book *Serious Mistranslations of the bible* demonstrating *GENEA* has two meanings well defined in the LXX. It means either "generation" or "race/peculiar group/related group/posterity" - I like to render "faithful family" since the family/related group is in view just like Young's "race" and the emphasis in quality is in context as a contrast to the preceding "unbelieving" who stumble at the rock of Jesus.

> But you *are* a faithful family, a royal priesthood, a holy
> nation, His own special people, that you may proclaim the
> praises of Him who called you out of darkness into His
> marvellous light;   *1 Peter 2:9 JM*

---

2 John 1:1

The Greek for "Lord" is *KURIOS* and the female counterpart *KURIA*
is found in 2 John 1:1 and 2 John 1:5. Some read this as a proper name
as Young does and translates it so. Again, as there is no simple straight
counterpart in English for "quality" as an adjective, a word that matches
the sentiment or meaning is needful. I choose "faithful" and Young as
we see has "choice".

> The Elder to the choice Kyria, and to her children, whom I
> love in truth, and not I only, but also all those having known
> the truth,   *2 John 1:1 YLT*

So that this,

> The Elder,
> To the elect lady and her children, whom I love in truth, and
> not only I, but also all those who have known the truth,
>   *2 John 1:1*

then, using the literal rendering for *EKLEKTOS*, becomes:

> The Elder,
> To the excellent lady and her children, whom I love in truth,
> and not only I, but also all those who have known the truth,
>   *2 John 1:1 JM*

---

2 John 1:13

Here I choose "faithful" and Young has picked "choice".

> Salute thee do the children of thy choice sister. Amen.
>   *2 John 1:13 YLT*

So that,

> The children of your elect sister greet you. Amen. *2 John 1:13*

then becomes,

> **The children of your faithful sister greet you. Amen.**
> *2 John 1:13 JM*

Revelation 17:14

The Young translation for *EKLEKTOS* is recognised as "choice" in various places and where he has used "chosen" or "elect" his notes (as mentioned in the preceding chapter) introducing the New Testament clarify that this should be read as "choice one" so that this thorough man of learning in regards to every Hebrew and Greek word of the bible as per his analytical concordance, he saw *EKLEKTOS* in a similar light to what I am claiming. He translates PISTOS as "stedfast" here (the older English version of "steadfast"), but this word which means "faithful" or "trustworthy" is more commonly associated with *PISTEUÓ* – "I believe". I like "steadfast" for *EKLEKTOS* as an alternative quality rendering since "faithful" is being used alongside. Here is Young:

> . . . these with the Lamb shall make war, and the Lamb shall overcome them, because Lord of lords he is, and King of kings, and those with him are called, and choice, and stedfast.
> *Revelation 17:14 Young*

So that,

> These will make war with the Lamb, and the Lamb will overcome them, for He is Lord of lords and King of kings; and those *who are* with Him *are* called, chosen, and faithful.
> *Revelation 17:14*

then becomes,

> These will make war with the Lamb, and the Lamb will overcome them, for He is Lord of lords and King of kings; and those with Him *are* called, steadfast, and faithful.
> *Revelation 17:14 JM*

CONCLUSION

The word "elect" (20) in the bible comes from either of 2 words: The Hebrew word BACHIR (13) in the Old Testament (OT) and the Greek word *EKLEKTOS* (23) in the New Testament (NT).

Other English words from these two source words in the KJV are "chosen" (15) and "choose" (1).
[20 + 15 + 1 = 13 + 23]

The Septuagint (LXX), the Greek version of the OT translated up to 3 centuries before Jesus, is quoted by the apostles in the NT. It was the OT read by the first Christians for about 4 centuries. The LXX gives us a different picture for *EKLEKTOS* and BACHIR.

The LXX only translates BACHIR by *EKLEKTOS* so the meaning of BACHIR according to the LXX translators is totally related to the meaning of *EKLEKTOS*.

The LXX shows 24 Hebrew words (occurring 594 times) as translated by *EKLEKTOS* on 74 occasions. The majority at first glance are fully seen as about "excellence": something of high quality.

The fat [*EKLEKTOS*] cows that came up out of the Nile in Pharaoh's dream which Joseph interpreted; the fat [*EKLEKTOS*] kernels of wheat in the same dream time; young men [*EKLEKTOS*] i.e. guys in their prime; to the pure [*EKLEKTOS*] You will show Yourself pure [*EKLEKTOS*]; pleasant [*EKLEKTOS*] land; pleasant [*EKLEKTOS*] jewels; desire [*EKLEKTOS*] of all nations; tried [*EKLEKTOS*] stone; precious [*EKLEKTOS*] clothes; choice [*EKLEKTOS*] silver; highest [*EKLEKTOS*] branch of the cedar; many more…

It is understandable then for a 1st century Christian who read:

"For many are called, but few *EKLEKTOS*" not to see,

For many are called, but few *are* chosen.   *Matthew 22:14*

But instead, it was natural to read,

For many are called, but few *have* mettle. *Matthew 22:14 JM*

With BACHIR only represented by *EKLEKTOS* in the LXX we can see the early church saw no meaning of "elect, chosen, selected" where it is found in most of today's English bibles, but the same as above.

There are 10 places where the Hebrew rendered as *EKLEKTOS* in the LXX, is given as "**chosen**" in the English (KJV).

A closer look at these 10 remaining by examining each of the four Hebrew words, BACHAR (6), MIBCHAR (2), BACHUR (1) and BARAR (1) then shows us these four are reasonably seen as also about high quality, not a "selected" idea. Not one of these then provides a reasonable doubt to the "top quality, excellent" meaning for *EKLEKTOS*.

BACHAR (172) is particularly revealing since it is the most used word in Hebrew for "to choose [X77], choosing, chosen [X77]". If *EKLEKTOS* has any realistic secondary meaning of "chosen, elect", then it is reasonable to see it with that emphasis in rendering BACHAR.

We see the primary use of BACHAR as "to choose, choosing, chosen" well rendered by such Greek words as *EKLEGÓ* (to choose, pick - 113), and *HAIRETIZÓ* (to choose - 12). But, in its secondary use as "to be chosen: preferred: excellent" BACHAR is rendered by such Greek words as *NEANIAS* (young man, youth - 4), *NEANISKOS* (young man, boy - 1) and *DUNATOS* (strong, mighty, able - 4): The use of *EKLEKTOS* (8) in rendering BACHAR is identical to these.

BACHUR (young man - 45) is also revealing in that *EKLEKTOS* (5) is the second most used word to translate it in the LXX after *NEANISKOS* (young man, boy - 34).

So with all occasions of *EKLEKTOS* as within the category of "best, top quality, excellent", a reasonable view can be seen that the LXX translators saw *EKLEKTOS* and thus BACHIR as about excellence: an indicator of high quality. As a result of the above observations there is no pointer to any occasion of *EKLEKTOS* in the LXX as meaning other than excellence.

Since we know the early Church all spoke Greek and read the LXX as their OT Scripture, let alone the Greek NT documents for the first three centuries of its existence – the Nicea Ecumenical Council of 325AD being all recorded in Greek an excellent pointer to that - then, we can reasonably see that the idea of (let alone the word) "elect" was never in their view, in any of the passages where it is found today in English bibles: The "excellent" were in view.

So, it is an etymological fact: There are no "elect" in the Bible.

WHAT YOU CAN DO

Paul wrote:

> **He Himself gave some *to be* apostles, some prophets, some evangelists, and some pastors and teachers, for the equipping of the saints for the work of ministry…** *Ephesians 4:11-12*

If you have read this book, you are now equipped.

In 2015 I wrote to both the Bible Society and Wycliffe Bible Translators in regards to this evidence. I sent both a copy of the full work represented in *Deleting ELECT in the Bible*.

Neither seemed interested in taking this seriously: as something they needed to do something about directly. James Poole the Wycliffe Director suggested the better approach was to inform the scholar community and I should try the publications they receive. The Bishop of London at the time was the President for the Bible Society and I wrote to him. He agreed with me to see this tested and sent it to a scholar he knew of. The following year, about ten months later, he wrote me to say he'd had no response from the scholar[1]. There is a journal entitled *The Bible Translator* which claims it "**is the leading academic journal dedicated to the theory and practice of Bible translation**". I attempted communication both with its Reviews Editor and its Executive Editor: neither responded. I also sent a copy of DEiTB and a letter to the Reviews Editor's address and also received no reply. So, I booked a full page advertising space with the publisher and submitted the artwork. At the last moment the Executive Director informed the publisher the ad would not be included. Though sought, no explanation was given.

This is merely to say I have played my part.

False teaching will continue in the Body of Christ for as long as we as saints continue to permit our source of belief, the bible, to be mistranslated in a manner to promote such heresy.

[1]See **http://www.jarom.net/bishopSEP2016.php** for the Bishop's final letter.

What you can do

You can pray.

You can share with your church leaders about this truth.

If you are a church leader, you can share with other church leaders you are acquainted with.

If you are a Bible Society or Translators Supporter: well done. Write to them and express your concern that they should inform their scholars and their translators the basic evidence. And, of course, whenever you come across a passage that is mistranslated, place a note in your bible. If you read it with others, explain why you see this differently.

We all need to play our part. Let's keep watch and see the truth grow.

List of Bible Passages
& Page Numbers

Genesis 1:11	60	Numbers 17:5	72
Genesis 1:12	60	Deuteronomy 1:25	60
Genesis 1:29	60	Deuteronomy 4:37	72
Genesis 3:2	60	Deuteronomy 6:13	19
Genesis 3:3	60	Deuteronomy 7:6	72
Genesis 3:6	60	Deuteronomy 7:7	72
Genesis 4:3	60	Deuteronomy 7:13	60
Genesis 6:2	72	Deuteronomy 10:15	72
Genesis 13:11	72	Deuteronomy 12:5	72
Genesis 23:6	16, 30-31, 81, 86	Deuteronomy 12:11	16, 72, 81-82, 86
Genesis 27:15	55	Deuteronomy 12:14	72
Genesis 30:2	60	Deuteronomy 12:15	62
Genesis 32:28	118	Deuteronomy 12:18	72
Genesis 41:2	16, 31, 47, 52	Deuteronomy 12:21	72
Genesis 41:4	16, 47, 48, 52	Deuteronomy 12:22	62
Genesis 41:5	16, 47, 48-49, 52	Deuteronomy 12:26	72
Genesis 41:7	16, 47, 49, 52	Deuteronomy 14:2	72
Genesis 41:18	16, 47, 49-50, 52	Deuteronomy 14:5	62
Genesis 41:20	16, 47, 50, 52	Deuteronomy 14:23	72
Genesis 43:34	57	Deuteronomy 14:24	72
Exodus 10:15	60	Deuteronomy 14:25	72
Exodus 14:7	16, 65-66, 72	Deuteronomy 15:20	72
Exodus 15:4	86, 99-100, 105	Deuteronomy 15:22	62
Exodus 15:20-21	116	Deuteronomy 16:2	72
Exodus 17:9	72	Deuteronomy 16:6	72
Exodus 18:25	72	Deuteronomy 16:7	72
Exodus 24:11	105	Deuteronomy 16:11	72
Exodus 30:23	16, 32, 56	Deuteronomy 16:15	72
Leviticus 19:23	60	Deuteronomy 16:16	72
Leviticus 19:24	60	Deuteronomy 17:8	72
Leviticus 19:25	60	Deuteronomy 17:10	72
Leviticus 23:40	60	Deuteronomy 17:15	72
Leviticus 25:10	56	Deuteronomy 18:5	72
Leviticus 25:19	60	Deuteronomy 18:6	72
Leviticus 26:4	60	Deuteronomy 20:19	58
Leviticus 26:20	60	Deuteronomy 20:20	58
Leviticus 27:30	60	Deuteronomy 21:5	72
Numbers 11:28	16, 32-33, 52	Deuteronomy 23:16	72
Numbers 12:3	117	Deuteronomy 26:2	60, 72
Numbers 13:20	60	Deuteronomy 26:10	60
Numbers 13:26	60	Deuteronomy 28:4	60
Numbers 13:27	60	Deuteronomy 28:11	60
Numbers 16:5	72	Deuteronomy 28:18	60
Numbers 16:7	72	Deuteronomy 28:33	60

Deuteronomy 28:42	60	2 Samuel 6:21	72
Deuteronomy 28:51	60	2 Samuel 10:9	72, 90, 92-93
Deuteronomy 28:53	58, 60	2 Samuel 11:8	57
Deuteronomy 28:55	58	2 Samuel 15:15	72
Deuteronomy 28:57	58	2 Samuel 16:18	72
Deuteronomy 30	117	2 Samuel 17:1	72
Deuteronomy 30:9	60	2 Samuel 19:38	72
Deuteronomy 30:19	72	2 Samuel 21:6	8, 16, 21-22, 114-115
Deuteronomy 31:11	72	2 Samuel 22:26-27	107
Deuteronomy 32:25	76, 96	2 Samuel 22:27	16, 33, 76, 80
Joshua 8:3	72	2 Samuel 23:5	56
Joshua 9:27	72	2 Samuel 24:12	72
Joshua 17:16	105	1 Kings 3:8	72
Joshua 17:18	105	1 Kings 4:23	16, 47, 50, 52, 62
Joshua 24:15	72	1 Kings 5:8	56
Joshua 24:22	72	1 Kings 5:9	56
Judges 3:17	52	1 Kings 5:10	56
Judges 5:8	72	1 Kings 8:16	72
Judges 10:14	72	1 Kings 8:44	72
Judges 14:10	76, 96	1 Kings 8:48	72
Judges 20:15	16, 65, 66-67, 72	1 Kings 9:11	56
Judges 20:16	72	1 Kings 10:13	56
Judges 20:34	16, 65, 67-68, 72	1 Kings 10:25	59
Judges 20:38	57	1 Kings 11:13	72
Judges 20:40	57	1 Kings 11:32	72
Ruth 3:10	76, 96	1 Kings 11:34	72
1 Samuel 2:28	72	1 Kings 11:36	72
1 Samuel 8:16	76, 96	1 Kings 12:21	72, 90
1 Samuel 8:18	72	1 Kings 14:21	72
1 Samuel 9:2	76, 96	1 Kings 18:23	72
1 Samuel 9:20	55	1 Kings 18:25	72
1 Samuel 10:24	72	2 Kings 3:19	58
1 Samuel 12:13	72	2 Kings 8:12	16, 33-34, 73, 76, 96
1 Samuel 13:2	72	2 Kings 10:2	59
1 Samuel 13:14	115	2 Kings 19:23	16, 34-35, 58
1 Samuel 15:22	56	2 Kings 19:24	58
1 Samuel 16:8	72	2 Kings 19:29	60
1 Samuel 16:9	72	2 Kings 19:30	60
1 Samuel 16:10	72	2 Kings 21:7	72
1 Samuel 17:40	72	2 Kings 23:27	72
1 Samuel 18:25	56	2 Kings 24:10	58
1 Samuel 20:30	72	2 Kings 25:2	58
1 Samuel 24:2	65, 68-69, 72	1 Chronicles 7:40	16, 76-77, 80
1 Samuel 24:3	16	1 Chronicles 9:22	16, 76, 77-78, 80, 98
1 Samuel 26:2	16, 65, 69-70, 72	1 Chronicles 12:8	62
2 Samuel 1:19	62	1 Chronicles 15:2	72
2 Samuel 2:18	62	1 Chronicles 16:13	8, 16, 21, 22, 114, 115
2 Samuel 6:1	72, 90	1 Chronicles 16:41	80, 98

1 Chronicles 19:10	72, 90, 93-94	Job 21:21	56
1 Chronicles 21:10	72	Job 22:3	56
1 Chronicles 28:4	72	Job 29:25	72
1 Chronicles 28:5	72	Job 31:16	56
1 Chronicles 28:6	72	Job 33:3	80
1 Chronicles 28:10	72	Job 34:4	72
1 Chronicles 29:1	72	Job 34:33	72
2 Chronicles 6:5	72	Job 36:21	72
2 Chronicles 6:6	72	Job 39:21	59
2 Chronicles 6:34	72	Job 41:30	53
2 Chronicles 6:38	72	Psalm 1:2	56
2 Chronicles 7:12	72	Psalm 1:3	60
2 Chronicles 7:16	72	Psalm 16:3	56
2 Chronicles 11:1	72, 90	Psalm 17:27	16
2 Chronicles 8:5	58	Psalm 18:26	76, 79, 80
2 Chronicles 9:12	56	Psalm 19:8	47
2 Chronicles 9:24	59	Psalm 21:10	60
2 Chronicles 11:5	58	Psalm 24:4	47
2 Chronicles 12:13	72	Psalm 25:12	72
2 Chronicles 13:3	72, 90	Psalm 31:21	58
2 Chronicles 13:17	72, 90	Psalm 33:12	72
2 Chronicles 20:25	55	Psalm 47:4	72
2 Chronicles 21:20	55	Psalm 58:11	60
2 Chronicles 24:6	57	Psalm 60:9	58
2 Chronicles 24:9	57	Psalm 65:4	72
2 Chronicles 25:5	72, 90	Psalm 68:13	53
2 Chronicles 29:11	72	Psalm 72:16	60
2 Chronicles 32:10	58	Psalm 73:1	47
2 Chronicles 32:27	55	Psalm 73:4	52
2 Chronicles 33:7	72	Psalm 77:31	16
2 Chronicles 36:10	55	Psalm 78:31	73-74, 76, 95, 96, 97
2 Chronicles 36:17	76, 96	Psalm 78:63	76, 96
Ezra 5:8	16, 35-36, 57	Psalm 78:67	72
Ezra 6:4	57	Psalm 78:68	72
Ezra 8:27	55	Psalm 78:70	72
Nehemiah 1:9	72	Psalm 84:3	56
Nehemiah 3:19	59	Psalm 84:10	72
Nehemiah 5:18	16, 76, 78-79, 80	Psalm 88:4	16
Nehemiah 9:7	72	Psalm 88:20	16
Nehemiah 9:36	60	Psalm 89:3	8, 21, 22-23, 114, 115
Nehemiah 10:35	60	Psalm 89:19	65, 70, 72
Nehemiah 10:37	60	Psalm 104:6	16
Esther 2:18	57	Psalm 104:13	60
Job 7:15	72	Psalm 104:43	16
Job 9:14	72	Psalm 105:5	16
Job 11:4	47	Psalm 105:6	8, 21, 23, 114, 115-116
Job 15:5	72	Psalm 105:23	16
Job 20:24	59	Psalm 105:26	72

Psalm 105:35	60	Proverbs 26:2	56
Psalm 105:43	8, 21, 23, 114, 116	Proverbs 27:18	60
Psalm 106:3	117	Proverbs 31:13	56
Psalm 106:5	8, 21, 24, 114, 116-117	Proverbs 31:16	60
Psalm 106:23	8, 21, 24-25, 114, 117	Proverbs 31:31	60
Psalm 106:24	55	Ecclesiastes 2:5	60
Psalm 107:30	56	Ecclesiastes 3:1	56
Psalm 107:34	60	Ecclesiastes 3:17	56
Psalm 107:37	60	Ecclesiastes 3:18	80
Psalm 111:2	56	Ecclesiastes 5:4	56
Psalm 119:30	72	Ecclesiastes 5:8	56
Psalm 119:173	72	Ecclesiastes 8:6	56
Psalm 127:3	60	Ecclesiastes 9:4	72
Psalm 132:11	60	Ecclesiastes 11:9	52, 76, 96
Psalm 132:13	72	Ecclesiastes 12:1	52, 56
Psalm 135:4	72	Ecclesiastes 12:10	56
Psalm 140:4	16	Song of Songs 2:3	60
Psalm 140:7	59	Song of Songs 2:7	62
Psalm 141:2	57	Song of Songs 2:9	62
Psalm 141:4	36	Song of Songs 2:17	62
Psalm 148:9	60	Song of Songs 3:5	62
Psalm 148:12	76, 96	Song of Songs 4:13	60
Proverbs 1:29	72	Song of Songs 4:16	60
Proverbs 1:31	60	Song of Songs 5:15	16, 65, 71, 72
Proverbs 3:14	53	Song of Songs 6:8	16
Proverbs 3:15	56	Song of Songs 6:9	16, 37-38, 46, 47
Proverbs 3:31	72	Song of Songs 6:10	46-47
Proverbs 6:5	62	Song of Songs 8:11	60
Proverbs 8:10	53, 72	Song of Songs 8:12	60
Proverbs 8:11	56	Song of Songs 8:14	62
Proverbs 8:19	16, 37, 53, 60, 65, 72	Isaiah 1:29	72
Proverbs 10:4	53	Isaiah 2:16;	55
Proverbs 10:20	72	Isaiah 3:10	60
Proverbs 11:30	60	Isaiah 4:2	60, 62
Proverbs 12:14	60	Isaiah 7:15	72
Proverbs12:24	16, 37, 53	Isaiah 7:16	72
Proverbs 12:27	53	Isaiah 9:17	76, 96
Proverbs 13:2	60	Isaiah 10:12	60
Proverbs 13:4	53	Isaiah 13:14	62
Proverbs 14:4	47	Isaiah 13:18	60
Proverbs 16:16	53, 72	Isaiah 13:19	62
Proverbs 18:20	60	Isaiah 14:1	72
Proverbs 18:21	60	Isaiah 14:29	60
Proverbs 20:29	76, 96	Isaiah 19:6	58
Proverbs 21:3	72	Isaiah 19:6	58
Proverbs 21:5	53	Isaiah 22:7	16, 81, 82-83, 86
Proverbs 22:1	72	Isaiah 22:8	16, 38-39, 59
Proverbs 25:21-22	20	Isaiah 23:4	76, 96

Isaiah 23:9	62	Isaiah 65:8	119
Isaiah 24:16	62	Isaiah 65:9	8, 16, 21, 26-27...
Isaiah 27:9	60	Isaiah 65:9	...114, 119
Isaiah 28:1	62	Isaiah 65:11-12	119
Isaiah 28:4	62	Isaiah 65:12	73
Isaiah 28:5	62	Isaiah 65:15	8, 16, 21, 27, 114, 119
Isaiah 28:16	16, 39-40, 128-129	Isaiah 65:21	60
Isaiah 28:27	53	Isaiah 65:22	8, 21, 28, 114, 119-120
Isaiah 31:8	76, 96	Isaiah 65:23	16
Isaiah 37:24	86	Isaiah 66:3	73
Isaiah 37:25	58	Isaiah 66:4	73
Isaiah 37:30	60	Jeremiah 2:7	60
Isaiah 37:31	60	Jeremiah 3:19	16, 40-41, 53, 55, 62
Isaiah 40:20	73	Jeremiah 4:11	80
Isaiah 40:30	76, 96	Jeremiah 6:1	57
Isaiah 41:8	73	Jeremiah 6:11	76, 96
Isaiah 41:9	73	Jeremiah 6:19	60
Isaiah 41:15	53	Jeremiah 7:20	60
Isaiah 41:24	73	Jeremiah 8:3	73
Isaiah 42:1	8, 16, 21, 25, 114...	Jeremiah 9:21	76, 96
Isaiah 42:1	...117-118	Jeremiah 10:17	16, 41, 58
Isaiah 42:6	117	Jeremiah 11:16	61
Isaiah 42:22	76, 96	Jeremiah 11:22	76, 96
Isaiah 43:10	73	Jeremiah 12:2	61
Isaiah 43:20	8, 16, 21, 25-26...	Jeremiah 12:10	55
Isaiah 43:20	...114, 118	Jeremiah 15:8	76, 96
Isaiah 43:21	118	Jeremiah 17:8	61
Isaiah 43:22-28	118	Jeremiah 17:10	61
Isaiah 44:1	73	Jeremiah 18:21	76, 96
Isaiah 44:2	73	Jeremiah 21:14	61
Isaiah 44:28	56	Jeremiah 19:9	58
Isaiah 45:4	8, 16, 21, 26, 114...	Jeremiah 22:7	16, 81, 83, 86
Isaiah 45:4	...118-119	Jeremiah 22:28	56
Isaiah 46:10	56	Jeremiah 25:34	53-54, 55
Isaiah 48:10	73	Jeremiah 29:5	61
Isaiah 48:14	56	Jeremiah 29:28	61
Isaiah 49:2	16, 76, 79-80	Jeremiah 31:13	76, 96
Isaiah 49:7	73	Jeremiah 31:15	16
Isaiah 52:11	80	Jeremiah 32:19	61
Isaiah 53:10	56	Jeremiah 32:34	16
Isaiah 54:12	16, 40, 56	Jeremiah 33:24	73
Isaiah 56:4	73	Jeremiah 34:8	57
Isaiah 58:3	56	Jeremiah 34:15	57
Isaiah 58:5	73	Jeremiah 34:17	57
Isaiah 58:6	73	Jeremiah 40:5	57
Isaiah 58:13	56	Jeremiah 48:15	76, 81, 83-84, 86...
Isaiah 61:1	56	Jeremiah 48:15	...96, 99, 100-101
Isaiah 62:5	76, 96	Jeremiah 48:38	56

Jeremiah 49:19	73	Ezekiel 31:3	61
Jeremiah 49:26	76, 96	Ezekiel 31:10	61
Jeremiah 50:30	76, 96	Ezekiel 31:14	61
Jeremiah 50:44	73	Ezekiel 31:16	17, 81, 84-85, 86
Jeremiah 51:3	76, 96	Ezekiel 34:27	61
Jeremiah 51:11	80	Ezekiel 36:8	61
Jeremiah 51:22	76, 96	Ezekiel 36:30	61
Jeremiah 52:5	58	Ezekiel 39:9	59
Lamentations 1:15	16, 73, 74-75, 76, 96	Ezekiel 39:10	59
Lamentations 1:18	76, 97	Ezekiel 34:3	52
Lamentations 2:14	57	Ezekiel 46:17	57
Lamentations 2:20	61	Ezekiel 47:12	61
Lamentations 2:21	76, 97	Daniel 1:15	52
Lamentations 5:13	16, 73, 75, 76, 97	Daniel 8:9	62
Lamentations 5:14	16, 73, 75-76, 97	Daniel 9:23	55
Ezekiel 4:2	58	Daniel 9:25	53
Ezekiel 4:3	58	Daniel 10:3	55
Ezekiel 4:7	58	Daniel 10:11	55
Ezekiel 4:8	58	Daniel 10:19	55
Ezekiel 5:2	58	Daniel 11:8	55
Ezekiel 7:20	17, 41-42, 61, 62	Daniel 11:15	17, 81, 85-86...
Ezekiel 7:22	17	Daniel 11:15	...99, 102-104
Ezekiel 9:6	76, 97	Daniel 11:16	62
Ezekiel 17:3	61, 106	Daniel 11:35	80
Ezekiel 17:8	61	Daniel 11:37	55
Ezekiel 17:9	61	Daniel 11:38	55
Ezekiel 17:22	42, 61	Daniel 11:41	62
Ezekiel 17:23	61	Daniel 11:43	55
Ezekiel 19:12	17, 42-43, 59, 61	Daniel 11:45	62
Ezekiel 19:14	17, 59-60, 61	Daniel 12:10	80
Ezekiel 20:5	73	Hosea 8:8	56
Ezekiel 20:6	62	Hosea 9:16	61
Ezekiel 20:15	62	Hosea 10:1	61
Ezekiel 20:38	80, 98-99	Hosea 10:13	61
Ezekiel 20:40	57	Hosea 13:15	55
Ezekiel 23:6	76, 97, 106	Hosea 14:8	61
Ezekiel 23:7	86, 99, 101-102, 106	Joel 2:22	61
Ezekiel 23:12	76, 97, 106	Joel 2:28	76, 97
Ezekiel 23:23	76, 97, 106	Joel 3:5	106
Ezekiel 24:4	86	Joel 3:14	53
Ezekiel 24:5	86, 106	Amos 1:3	53
Ezekiel 25:4	61	Amos 2:9	61
Ezekiel 25:9	17, 61-62	Amos 2:11	76, 97
Ezekiel 26:12	55	Amos 4:10	76, 97
Ezekiel 26:20	62	Amos 5:11	17, 44-45, 57
Ezekiel 27:20	17, 43	Amos 6:12	61
Ezekiel 27:24	17, 43-44	Amos 8:13	76, 97
Ezekiel 30:17	76, 97	Amos 9:14	61

Micah 5:1	58	Mark 13:20	. . .122-123
Micah 6:4	116	Mark 13:22	8, 120, 123
Micah 6:7	61	Mark 13:27	8, 120, 123
Micah 7:12	58	Luke 2:32	117
Micah 7:13	61	Luke 4	15
Nahum 2:9	55	Luke 4:8	19
Nahum 3:14	58	Luke 18:7	8, 120, 123
Habakkuk 1:16	17, 48, 51, 52	Luke 23:35	8, 120, 124
Habakkuk 2:1	58	John 4:35	12
Zephaniah 3:9	80	Acts 10:34-35	125
Zephaniah 3:18	57	Acts 17:11	15
Haggai 2:7	17, 53, 54, 55	Romans 2:6-16	126
Haggai 2:23	73	Romans 8:33	8, 120, 124, 125
Zechariah 1:3	53	Romans 12:19-20	19
Zechariah 1:17	73	Romans 16:13	8, 120, 124
Zechariah 2:12	73	Ephesians 4:11-12	135
Zechariah 3:2	73	Colossians 3:12	8, 120, 125
Zechariah 7:14	17, 53, 54-55	1 Timothy 3:16	117-118
Zechariah 8:12	61	1 Timothy 2:3-4	12
Zechariah 9:3	58	1 Timothy 4:1	12, 15
Zechariah 9:17	76, 97	1 Timothy 5:21	8, 120, 125
Zechariah 11:16	17, 48, 51-52	2 Timothy 2:10	8, 120, 125-126
Zechariah 12:2	58	Titus 1:1	8, 120, 126
Malachi 1:10	56	Titus 1:1-2	126
Malachi 3:11	61	1 Peter 1	14
Malachi 3:12	56	1 Peter 1:1	109, 120
Matthew 4	15	1 Peter 1:1-2	14, 109-110, 126-128
Matthew 4:10	19	1 Peter 1:2	8, 120
Matthew 9:37-38	12	1 Peter 2:4	8, 120, 128
Matthew 18:4	117	1 Peter 2:6	8, 120, 128-129
Matthew 20:16	8, 120, 121	1 Peter 2:9	8, 120, 129-130
Matthew 22:14	8, 45, 120, 121, 133	2 John 1:1	8, 63, 120, 130
Matthew 24:22	8, 120, 121, 122	2 John 1:5	130
Matthew 24:24	8, 121-122, 123	2 John 1:13	8, 120, 130-131
Matthew 24:31	8, 120, 122, 123	Revelation 2:15	12
Mark 13:20	8, 120, 121. . .	Revelation 17:14	8, 120, 131